One Day *He Beckoned*

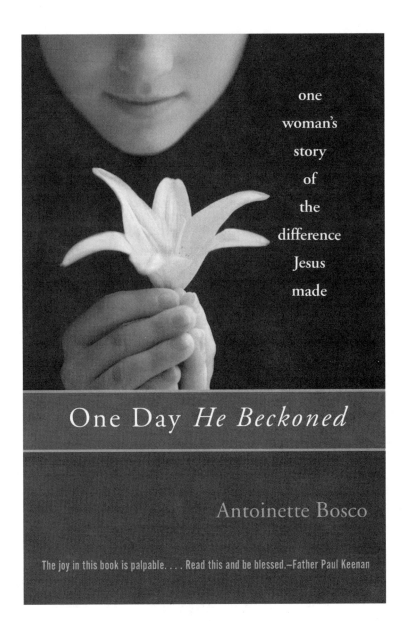

one
woman's
story
of
the
difference
Jesus
made

One Day *He Beckoned*

Antoinette Bosco

The joy in this book is palpable. . . . Read this and be blessed.–Father Paul Keenan

ave maria press™ AmP Notre Dame, Indiana

© 2004 by Ave Maria Press,™ Inc.

All rights reserved. No part of this book may be used or reproduced in any manner whatsoever, except in the case of reprints in the context of reviews, without written permission from Ave Maria Press, Inc., P.O. Box 428, Notre Dame, IN 46556.

www.avemariapress.com

International Standard Book Number: 0-87793-999-3

Cover and text design by Katherine Robinson Coleman

Printed and bound in the United States of America

Library of Congress Cataloging-in-Publication Data is available.

I joyfully dedicate this book to my sister, Dr. Jeannette Oppedisano, who has always brought happiness, laughter, and wisdom into my life and who has been a blessing to all of us in her devotion to family, her compassion for one who is hurting, and her generosity in all ways. I have no words that can do justice to the reality of her goodness.

Contents

Acknowledgments

The writing of every book begins with a story. This one originates with a phone call from John Kirvan, a writer of great spiritual books. He called me to discuss the possibility of my writing a book for a special series on faith-based practices he is editing for the publisher. I didn't think the topic he suggested was quite the right one for me at this time. But in our conversation I told him the one spiritual book I would be interested in writing would be on how Jesus shaped my life.

We talked more and John suggested I write a proposal on what such a book would cover. He said he would look at it and then send it to Ave Maria Press editorial director Bob Hamma. I was delighted to do this.

Well, a writer writes, and I, going beyond a proposal, sent him an introduction and first chapter. Within a couple of weeks, I received a call from Bob Hamma with the affirming news that they wanted to publish my story, telling me that Dan Driscoll would be my editor. This marked the beginning of not just a professional relationship, but a friendship. I am so grateful for this opportunity to express my gratitude to John and Bob (and Dan) for their confidence in me.

I am also grateful to my five children, their spouses, my fifteen grandchildren, and my seven brothers and sisters for their unwavering support for me and always their expressed appreciation of my writing, which puts me on a humble ego trip!

Mostly, I am grateful for having had the blessed good fortune of being born into a family where I would be put in touch with Jesus, who gave me the meaning of my life.

ANTOINETTE BOSCO, Brookfield, Connecticut

Introduction

I was fifteen when I learned that Jesus has his own unique ways of getting your attention. It was a Saturday morning in early spring and I had gone uptown with my mother in my hometown of Albany, New York. That wasn't my choice, it was my mother's. She didn't want to be alone that day because she didn't know the uptown area very well. She usually went shopping downtown where the larger stores, and many more of them, were located.

Well, I had a lot of homework to do and I wasn't particularly thrilled over having to go shopping with my mother, who always took hours to find what she liked. I would survive these shopping days by daydreaming, usually about a book or some creative school project I was planning. Very often these thoughts would have a religious theme because I was very involved with my teachers, the Sisters of St. Joseph of Carondelet. In fact, it had been my practice since my early school years to go to my beloved cathedral, the Church of the Immaculate Conception, every morning for Mass.

I was standing still as my mother was busy looking at some clothes in a store window when I suddenly felt drawn to focus on the block ahead of me. Strangely, I had a mental image of Jesus, pouring out love from his Sacred Heart. He was in profile, looking down, with his right hand extended in welcome. But it was his left hand that drew me, beckoning me to come to him.

I began running down the block, and suddenly I stopped. I was in front of a religious goods store that I had no way of knowing was located there, since I hadn't ever been in that precise area before. I looked at the statues, the rosaries, and the prayer books in the window I first faced, but then, turning to the right window, I remember I literally gasped. There, on the wall, was an eight-by-ten framed plaque of Jesus that I had just "seen" in a strange but vibrant visualization a block away. From high up on that wall, it was as if Jesus was looking down at me, clearly beckoning me. I was mesmerized.

By this time, my mother had reached me. She started yelling at me, something like "What's the matter with you? What were you running for?"

I knew if I told her I had "seen" a picture of Jesus beckoning to me, and truly had no idea why I started running, she, logically, could think I was a nut case. So I played it safe, and told her I wanted to see the holy items in this store. She had no problem with my going in. I wasted no time. I asked the man at the desk immediately how much the plaque in the window cost. He said $2.50. That was a lot of money for me back then. I had fifty cents in my purse. I asked him if he would hold it for me if I put a fifty-cent deposit on it. He said yes, and generously gave me one month to raise the rest of the money. I was thrilled.

Actually, I didn't have to wait that long. I told my father about this beautiful picture of Jesus that I had seen, and he gave me the two dollars to go get it without waiting. I remember how I hugged it as I carried it home, and hung it on a nail on the wall in my bedroom. I would think sometimes of how strange it had been that I had actually "seen" this image of Jesus before it was humanly possible to have really seen it, or to know that it was in the religious goods store. In my youthful way, I took this as a sign that Jesus was calling me, that he beckoned to me because I was special, good, and holy.

Ah, how nice it is to be young, untried, unwounded by life, sure of yourself, sure of your strength, and still protected from having to drink of the chalice in the garden of Gethsemane. I was, rather soon, to learn a different lesson from my gift of the image. It had been given to me not because I was deserving of a special grace, but because I would need a special grace to survive my life without despair. And that special grace was to be able to look at that image of Jesus, being constantly reminded that he was beckoning me, assuring me that no matter what I was going through in my life, he would be there to hold me with his extended right hand as he never stopped beckoning to me with his left. All I had to do was believe him and follow him.

That plaque of Jesus has been on the wall next to my bed for nearly sixty years, through twelve moves from towns and cities as I completed my education during wartime, married and raised a family, endured a divorce, and faced the tragic deaths of two sons, a daughter-in-law, and so many loved ones. I never ever saw another plaque, or even a drawing, like this one. It was, and is, a gift, but it came with a challenge. That hand of Jesus, beckoning me, raised valid questions. Who would I be following? Who is this Jesus who wants me to take his hand? Who would I become if I trusted him so surely? And did he hold his hand out to others as powerfully as he did to me? Bottom line—he caught my attention in a way that cannot be explained scientifically, but catch it he did, permanently.

As for what I learned about him, let me summarize.

Of all the good people who have made an impact on the world, one alone stands out as different and absolutely unique—Jesus.

Sometimes he has been reduced to the category of a nice teacher of moral values.

He has been praised, admired, vilified, hated, followed, rejected, loved, and cursed.

He has been denied and re-crucified. Yet, he has never been put to death for keeps. Jesus lives.

Back in the 1950s, when Archbishop Fulton Sheen had his weekly TV show, he made a comment about Jesus that I'll never forget. The eminent speaker said that Jesus was so unique that he "split time into B.C. and A.D." (Before Christ and "In the year of our Lord").

No matter what a person believes or doesn't believe, no one can deny, said Cambridge theologian C.H. Dodd, that with the coming of Jesus, "A whole new era in relations between God and man had set in."

God intervened in human history in the person of Jesus and the world would never be the same again.

People can accept or reject Jesus, but the overwhelming evidence, both in his lifetime and in the centuries following, is that once, and only once, did the world experience such a person.

Jesus was different, and the two things that made him unique in his lifetime were his message and what he said about himself. He was a person who had a powerful effect on people. He spoke with authority about his "Father" and his "kingdom," and miraculously changed the natural order of things—to cure the sick, give sight to the blind, raise people from the dead, and bring them back to life.

He preached a strange message of how people should live with love, which was radically different from all the pragmatic eye-for-an-eye teachings of the past.

His message was strange for the world of his time, precisely because it was unworldly. He didn't come with a do-it-yourself kit on how to make it comfortably as a Jew in the discomforting hands of the Romans, a message most of his countrymen would have preferred and probably understood.

Instead, Jesus continually spoke of God, calling him our "Father"—in fact, our "Daddy"—and insisting that everything about humans makes sense only when we are plugged into the Kingdom of God.

What was even more shocking was Jesus' proclamation that the Kingdom of God was happening NOW, that the decisive turning point in human history was here. Salvation was theirs, but not for the *asking*, only for the *doing*, in love, as Jesus himself was demonstrating.

Even the poor had the gospel—the "good news"— preached to them. And this was the news—that God had intervened in human events to let his people know their purpose in life; that he is a Father, loving, generous, and forgiving; that the good person is the one who lives in keeping with the Father's word, accepting the mystery of God's promise that, in the end, life will triumph over death.

This was the most jarring piece of Good News that could fall on human ears, because to accept it meant that a person had to change radically, and change is discomforting and painful.

In his specific teachings about how people should live, Jesus shattered the sacred cows of pious externals and pointed out that the Kingdom of God begins on the inside, in the heart of humans, in their conversion to love.

Even in the other teaching method he used, the parables, Jesus never let up on the message—that God is intrinsically bound up with persons even in all the ordinary aspects of their lives, that the Kingdom of God is related to everyday events.

If the message was strangely topsy-turvy to a legalistic people, a repudiation of all the familiar power-patterns in exchange for a Kingdom "not of this world," even more difficult to grasp was the unprecedented way in which Jesus identified himself with the message.

In effect, what he said was that God was personified in him, was uniquely present in him, and that when people experience him, they experience the Father, who is present in him. No wonder he was vilified for blasphemy!

Yet, for all that Jesus did identify himself in a messianic role, he was immensely human. What's more, he lived his message, accepting and forgiving even the despised sinners of the time, like the adulteress and the tax collector. He took on the familiar struggles faced by all human beings—hunger, fatigue, rejection, disillusionment, decision-making, death, yet remained ever-compassionate, never backing off from his bottom line urging—"Love one another."

Finally, mysteriously, he accepted the ultimate act of love—to lay down one's life for one's friends. Only for Jesus this was not a final gift, but a forever gift, holding to an unbreakable promise that he, and all who believed in him, would live forever.

Who was this Jesus that he could say and do these things? I have asked that question all my life, joining those who have asked this question for over two thousand years of Christian history. Interestingly, the very first person to raise the question was Jesus himself. It is recorded in all three synoptic gospels, Matthew, Mark, and Luke, that Jesus put this blunt question to his disciples, "Who do people say I am? Who do *you* say I am?"

From the early days of the church, the pendulum has swung from these three poles—the Arians, who said Jesus was only a man; the Docetists, who said that he was not really human, had no real body, and was only divine, and those who followed Athanasius, who proclaimed that Jesus was both God and human. The debate over the question of whether Jesus was only human or only divine went on for four centuries, until finally, at the Council of Chalcedon in 451, the church spoke, dogmatically settling the question in proclaiming that Jesus Christ was of "two natures," both fully God and fully human, with no over-emphasis to be placed on either his divinity or his humanity.

But while the divinity/humanity debate was dogmatically settled by the church, in the actual everyday search by people for God over the centuries, the question is far from forever-resolved. Each baptized Christian still finds the day arrives when he or she must ask personally: Who is Jesus: God, man, or both?

The two-thousand-year-old choice is still the same today—to settle for calling Jesus a good person, a great religious leader, and saying that all that is important is how you live out his moral teachings; or to accept the fact that Jesus did identify himself in a messianic role, saying that he IS the Christ, the expression of God in human terms and the bearer of the "good news" from God, and that if human persons could believe in an unseen kingdom that begins in their hearts and minds and stretches out to infinity, they could live forever.

The choice is rooted in belief and it is a person's faith that determines if he or she can accept that Jesus is God. The late theologian, Paul Tillich, put it well: "Christianity was born, not with the birth of the man called Jesus, but in the moment in which one of his followers was driven to say to him, 'Thou art the Christ.'"

Perhaps the hardest thing for us to understand is why it should matter to Jesus/God that we follow him. We can easily fall into a dark place that makes us wonder if we have any importance at all, given the vastness of creation and the billions of human persons born into this vastness down through the ages. But that, of course, is where Jesus comes in, really comes in, to destroy our doubts. With his birth and his flesh and blood life, just like ours, Jesus/God started a traffic between two worlds that never existed before, preaching a strange message radically different from all the pragmatic, power-drenched teachings of the past— that the ticket to the good life in both worlds is love, and he holds the ticket.

It took me a long time to really understand that Jesus beckoned me when I was still a teenager to offer me something I would need. It was that precious ticket. But it wouldn't be free; I'd have to earn it with utter fidelity. My choice. This is what I've learned and what I relearn every morning when I get out of bed and look at the image of Jesus on my wall that I first "saw" without my eyes six decades ago.

I

The Assignment *Jesus Accepted*

---

*"I believe in Christianity as I believe in
the sun—not only because I see it, but
because by it I see everything else."*

—C. S. LEWIS

If anyone asked me at that untried age of fifteen about my relationship with Jesus, I would have waxed eloquently about "my love affair with Jesus." I woke up every morning hearing the full-toned bells of my great cathedral ringing, calling me to morning Mass. When there was a bright morning sun, I would walk up the long center aisle, basking in the rays that would make jewels out of the many gorgeous stained glass windows and bring life to the gold leaf tones of the five altars. The cathedral was so mysterious to me in these quiet morning hours that I used to feel as if I had entered infinity and found a timeless world.

I read about cathedrals and found that I had understood quite precisely what a cathedral is, a monument to infinity. Even the building of this cathedral had a romanticism about it that captivated me. It had begun as a dream in the mind of Father John McClosky, a thirty-seven-year-old priest, installed as the first Bishop of Albany, New York. on September 19, 1847. He hoped to have a cathedral modeled after a great one in Europe, and immediately found a site. It was an undeveloped area a bit removed from the city proper. People called this place "Gallows Hill" because nearby was the site formerly used for the execution of criminals. In my later daydreaming I liked to believe that perhaps the bishop had chosen this site precisely so that it could now become holy ground.

When it came time to begin the actual building, Bishop McClosky sent out an appeal to his priests: "Will you please notify your people that we are about to begin the work of excavation at the cathedral, that we hope to have it done by gratuitous labor, and that there will not be wanting those among your congregation who will cheerfully devote two or three days to the work. Those who can bring horse and cart will confer a great favor by doing so."

That is how the cathedral was built, by the labor of people, many of whom at the end of their day's work would go to the site to work into the night hours to build this monument to the Lord. In the end, the building, named the Cathedral of the Immaculate Conception, with its high altar, its tremendous center aisle, its deeply bright-colored stained glass windows, its huge organ and elegant rose window was indeed patterned after a magnificent edifice in Europe, the Cathedral of Notre Dame in Paris.

I spent countless hours in my cathedral, many of them just sitting in the church, reading the lives of the saints. I was fascinated by these extraordinary religious men and women who were so drenched in the love of God that they had a connection with him that we ordinary mortals can hardly image let alone grasp with any true understanding. The mystics, who seemed to have extraordinary personal contact with the Lord, were especially appealing.

Of course, I didn't know at that time that I really didn't comprehend what the saints were actually all about. As any teenager in a normal state of immaturity might conclude, I thought they were telling me it was noble to despise our lowly human condition, and that we were here on earth to purge ourselves of our despicable imperfections which kept us from seeking total completion in God.

My first real dose of reality came when I read Jacopone da Todi and tried to relate to what he said: "Send me illness, O Lord. . . . Chills every day and swollen dropsy. Give me toothache, headache and stomach cramps. . . . Let my mouth be full of ulcerous sores. . . ." And the plagues he wanted went on and on until he came to the punch line: "For you created me as your beloved, and I, ungrateful wretch, put you to death."

That's when I decided to look again at what Jesus had to say about how we should live, and it didn't surprise me in the least that he hadn't advocated such self-centered masochism. I had already found what struck me as the most challenging message to come from Jesus, in Matthew 25, where he lets us know, in no uncertain terms, how we should live. We should feed the hungry, give drink to the thirsty, visit the prisoners, take care of the sick. How could we ever do any of that if we were self-centeredly begging for physical ailments so we could punish ourselves for what happened to Jesus instead of doing the good works that would keep him "alive" in this world? That was the end of my affair with the Jacopone da Todi type of holiness!

I had already learned something about doing good works from my father back in 1936 when I was all of seven years old, though, of course, it was a bit later when I was mature enough to internalize the full impact of what he had done. My father, who loved music, had come home from work and with evident excitement told me and my sister Rosemary, who was two years older, that he had a wonderful surprise for us. He was getting us a piano.

This was the Depression era and somehow my father, Joseph Oppedisano, who made thirty-five dollars a week as a butcher in a meat and grocery market in downtown Albany, had managed to save twenty-five dollars, the cost of a second-hand upright piano. Then, three days before the piano was to be delivered, he waited on a customer, an old woman. Her purchase came to one dollar. Somewhat embarrassed, she asked my father if he could cut her meat by a few ounces to make it come to ninety cents. All she had was one dollar and she needed ten cents for the bus to get home.

My father, feeling for her, gave her the one dollar package, charging her ninety cents. She thanked him, and when she turned away, he took ten cents out of his own pocket and put it into the cash register to make up the difference. All the while, his boss had been watching. When the woman was out of hearing range, he literally bellowed at my father that this was no way to run a store. Business was business. Charity was something else, and not allowed in his store.

My father, a proud and kind man, not believing what he was hearing, responded that he couldn't work for a man who had no heart. He quit his job then and there. I remember him coming home early from work that day. I can still visualize his dejection when he told us the piano wasn't coming. He had a wife and two children to support. The twenty-five dollars he had saved for the piano was what we had to live on until he found another job. I was so disappointed, but yet, so proud of my father. Even at a very young age, I could imagine that Jesus would have done the very same thing, though I couldn't have yet known how my father's goodness, shown to me when I was still impressionable, would shape me more and more as I got older.

Well, these first fifteen years were my "honeymoon" time with Jesus and life. I was tops in school; my mother and dad had decided to let God determine the size of their family and I now had two young brothers and a baby sister who brought me nothing but joy; my father had his own meat market now and I often worked with him, enjoying how he always made his customers feel good; my older sister, Rosemary, and I had discovered the heavenly world of classical music, and we had a piano and two accordions in the house; and I had my daily destination at my cathedral where I could comfortably pray. Almost best of all, I had now been somewhat miraculously "visited" in the uptown Albany shopping area by my Lord Jesus, who had sent me his picture, beckoning me. It was my assurance, now affixed on my bedroom wall, that life was, and would remain, good.

What I didn't know was that, at age fifteen, my "good" life was about to change, from the inside out. We were in the throes of World War II and like everyone else my age, I had been contributing to the war effort. I worked in my father's "victory garden;" made sure the shades were drawn every night so no light escaped to let enemy planes that may have entered our skies see light; removed the tops and bottoms of cans so they could be flattened and the metal returned to the defense effort; sang patriotic songs; applauded patriotic movies; and cheered our high-school boys who dropped out of school to become soldiers, sailors, and marines.

It was in my cathedral that I was pummeled with a dose of reality and felt the sobering pain of war, at a morning Mass when a funeral was in progress. I could see the flag-draped coffin, and hear the screams of the mother, who the priest called a "Gold Star Mother." Her son had been killed in action. I knew about war deaths. I had seen this in the movies. I never knew I would see the pain up close.

A few days later I was reading the daily paper when I froze. It carried a full page of photos unlike any I could ever have imagined. Somehow, reporters had gotten hold of these in Europe somewhere. They were of a Jewish prisoner of the Germans being gassed to death. There were maybe six rows of frames showing the man reacting to the gas being poured into him, until the final photo where his head was down and he had finally, mercifully, died.

I was shaking and crying. Was this what war was all about? Mercilessly killing another? Why hadn't we heard about what was happening to the Jews in Europe? How could this have happened? I began to read everything I could find about the war. Then, the Masses for the Dead increased as more and more of our killed servicemen came back to us in body bags. Now it was too close to home, as I mourned the deaths of boys I had known in school.

I talked to my father about the horror of war, and for the first time, he told me he knew about war, for he was a boy of twelve when World War I dragged most of the countries of Europe into a senseless bloodbath lasting four years and ultimately causing the deaths of some fifty million people. He lived in a poor town in Calabria in Italy. There was always a shortage of food there and sometimes it was only because of having olives to eat that people survived.

When the war erupted in Italy, food had to be available for the soldiers. The villagers were at the mercy of the military, for the soldiers had the authority to come into a home, take all the food there, and leave. It didn't matter if children would be left to starve. My father told me, with tears running down his cheeks, how he and his father, in the dark of the night, crawled way out into a field dragging some sacks of food and a shovel. Praying that they wouldn't be discovered, they dug a hole, buried the food, and covered the fresh dirt with twigs, stones, and rubble to make it look untouched.

When the soldiers came for food, his father gave them everything left in the house and they went away. But thanks to the buried supplies, they, a family of five, survived the winter. It was then that my father, all of thirteen years old, said he decided to leave his homeland and try to make it to America. It was a difficult passage. It took him three years to work his way up through Italy and France in wartime until he finally could make a deal to get on a boat to America. He was then sixteen.

Then my father told me another story, this one about being in France, and starving. He started to cry as he told me about hunger and how he had stolen a loaf of bread, the first time he ever stole anything in his life. It seared him that he had to steal to keep himself from starvation. It was like a light went on. I had worked with him in his meat market and had seen something impressive, his generosity. I doubt if there was a day in his working life that he didn't give food to a hungry person. Now I knew why, and I honored him for not having become cynical from the horrors of war. More so, I felt such admiration for his endurance and for how he had, consciously or not, fed the hungry ever since, as Jesus would have done.

When my father died in 1985 at age eighty-three, my brother Joe stood up at the end of the Mass and gave a spontaneous eulogy for our father, who had spent most of his life working hard for his family of eight children, and through his business literally feeding the poor. I expected Joe to talk about Dad's many kindnesses, and he did. But then he said, "and let's talk about the gift of music," pointing out the many there, children and grandchildren, who are musicians. Then he asked, "But who sang the first song?"

Tears welled up in me for my brother's question had peeled away fifty years, bringing me back to the day we almost had a piano, except for ten cents. I remembered how my immigrant father, then thirty-three, was so drawn to music that the only money he had been able to save was to be spent on a piano, to pass on his love for the harmonies of song to his young daughters.

Yet, he had put a greater importance on the pervasive harmony that should be shared by all human beings—namely caring—even if it is a stranger who only needs a dime. When my brother asked, "Who sang the first song?" I could have shouted, "Our father did." For not only did he give us the gift of music, he sang a ten-cent song that forever resounded in our hearts.

I had come to believe that when goodness is done as Jesus urged, this is not a brief moment that will be forgotten. It will spread like a benediction reaching others. My father's goodness underscored that. But I learned that there is another side, a dark one. When cruelty and evil are done, sometimes couched in the lie of being justified, by governments as well as individuals, this, too, can spread.

As I became immersed in the daily news stories of the war in my teen years, I felt an ever-increasing horror of how war justifies death. I learned something terrifying—that "man's inhumanity to man" still characterized humankind. And I confronted God, demanding to know why he wasn't fixing all the things wrong with his world.

I think God got back to me in his own, individual way. I happened to be reading some works by Gilbert Chesterton, the British writer who had converted to Catholicism. He was high on creation and nature, and God's ways. What I most was struck by, though, was the point he made about Jesus. Chesterton challenged what the poet Robert Browning wrote, that "God's in his heaven, all's right with the world." No, the writer mused, he's wrong. If all were right with the world, God wouldn't have had to send his son *to show us how to make the world right.*

That was the truth, and it took root in me. That was Jesus' assignment. His Father had sent him into our world *to show us how to make the world right!*

Now as I looked at the picture of Jesus, beckoning to me, I understood its meaning. He was inviting me to take on his assignment. I felt inspired, but scared to death.

2

The Road Map *for Heaven*

I never spoke with God,

Nor visited in Heaven;

Yet certain am I of the spot

As if the chart were given.

—EMILY DICKINSON

Istarted college at age sixteen with excitement in September 1945. The terrible war was over, and we felt a kind of rebirth, rejoicing every time the newspapers carried a story of a serviceman's homecoming. As for my personal situation, it was great. I had gotten a good scholarship making it possible for me to attend the College of St. Rose in my hometown of Albany. Going here had been my goal because this college had been founded by the Sisters of St. Joseph of Carondelet, the same order of nuns who had staffed my high school, the Cathedral Academy. It was much later in my life that I recognized the great impact they had, especially Sister Anna Theresa, the librarian, who gave me a treasure before she died, her little black book of writings. In it I found her favorite saying, "A hot head seems so much more pardonable than a cold heart." And she would talk about Jesus, how he never had a cold heart, and all we had to do to get to heaven was to be like him. She didn't have to convince me. I already knew that, like I knew everything at sixteen.

At St. Rose, we used to have Wednesday afternoon assembly meetings, when a speaker would be brought in to talk to us about various subjects, from faith to politics, and we would try to stay awake.

Well, one Wednesday, the speaker was this handsome young priest, Father James Keller, and we all stayed awake! You couldn't help it. He had just completed a book, *You Can Change the World*, and was mesmerizing us with his enthusiasm about how we each had it in us *to change the world*. Specifically, he pointed us to three professions where we could make that kind of difference—politics, teaching, and writing.

I was a pre-med student, hoping desperately to get to medical school after graduation. Yet, I was always writing. I had been my high school's correspondent for *The Evangelist*, the Albany Catholic weekly, and even could brag of having had poetry published. When Father Keller said we could change the world by our writing, he really got my attention. Still, I wasn't planning on being a writer. I wanted to be a doctor, become a Maryknoll nun, and go to China, or someplace, to deliver and take care of babies.

I was already very experienced in taking care of babies. My mother, who had been unaware that practicing birth control was in violation of church laws, was set straight about this by my Aunt Mary who told her she'd go to hell if she did something "artificial" to avoid having children. Mom panicked. My father was overjoyed. All he had ever wanted was a lot of children. I couldn't count the times he told me when I worked in his meat market with him, "Antoinette, all that's important is a big family and a clear conscience." I was twelve, my sister Rosemary was fourteen, and my brother Joe was eight when the babies started coming, three of them by the time I started college, with two more born before I graduated. What we didn't know was that Mom, who was manic-depressive, would have to depend on us to take over much of the care of the babies.

Those babies were our joy, and I was convinced that I wanted to help bring loads of them into the world, as a good doctor. I felt I had the approval of Jesus, who spoke so lovingly about children. None of my college friends had baby brothers and sisters, so I knew I was different, but that only made me feel special. Reinforcing this was the affirmation my sister Rosemary and I had received at the cathedral from wonderful Sister Helena. She helped us to deal with the strict Italian rules we lived with at home, which made it impossible for us to be involved with any extracurricular school activities and caused us to be the occasional butt of sneers and snide remarks from certain classmates. Sister Helena, who had been teaching for fifty years or more, was wisdom personified. She told us not to be concerned about people who would make fun of you or unfairly criticize you when you know you are doing what is right. She respected our obedience. Her words to us, like a Jesus teaching, were "Dare to be different, and be proud that you are." So I was proud to be the unique college student who was the big sister of a houseful of great little ones.

I was a sophomore when my mother gave birth to Loretta. She was still in the hospital when I was called out of a biology class to answer a phone call. It was my father, calling me from his meat market. He was kind of laughing, telling me that I had a job to do because he didn't have the car. That morning, for some reason or other, I had requested and he had allowed me to take the car to school. Now he had gotten a call from my mother saying she wanted to come home from the hospital with the baby and the doctor had said yes. I had the car, so I was the driver! I still remember the awe I felt, carrying that gorgeous baby girl to the car, pointing out to my mother that her lips were like a rose bud, and she would have to give her two names, Loretta Rose.

The joke ever after among my college friends was that I was the only student who ever came up with such a novel reason for getting out of a biology class!

Being poor and female were not good qualifications for getting into medical school in 1948. Added to those negatives was my father's problem. He really wanted me to fulfill my dream of becoming a doctor, but he was from southern Italy, and in his culture, no father would let his daughter leave home unless she was married. He told me, I know with incredible sadness, that "God made a mistake. You should have been a boy." I would have to forget medical school. In fact, he had arranged a marriage for me.

The day after I had to face this reality, I went to Mass as was my custom, asking Jesus over and over to help me cope. Before I went to class I stopped at the St. Rose library. I happened to pick up a book of the writings of St. Francis de Sales and saw to my surprise that he was the patron saint of journalists and writers. The book oddly enough opened to a page with a story about St. Francis coming across a discouraged man walking along a row of blooming roses, complaining, "Isn't it a shame that roses have thorns." St Francis saw something else. "No, rather, isn't it wonderful that thorns have roses." At that point, my life was full of thorns. But those words of St. Francis had a profound effect on me. They flipped me out of despair. They became a theme for my life. I had never forgotten what Father Keller had said about writers. Now I believed that St. Francis de Sales, the patron saint of writers, had given me a message—that there were roses ahead if I pursued the path of becoming a writer.

Fast forward many years and I could say, with much gratitude, that I followed Father Keller's advice and chose writing as my way to do what he challenged us to do—to light the candles, and not curse the darkness, to affirm, always, the life-giving values of the human spirit. By the time Father Keller died in 1977, his Christ-bearing message of hope had encircled the world, brilliantly—and determined the path of my life.

I say that in all seriousness because my writing was never done just to make a living—though, indeed, I had to do that, supporting myself and my six children. My arranged marriage was a disaster, ending in 1967, but it brought me those children, the greatest blessings a person could have.

I remember an unbelievably difficult Saturday in January 1968 when I discovered, in a profound way, the road map to heaven. I was a reporter with *The Long Island Catholic* diocesan newspaper, but I always needed to earn more money to support such a large family, and so I wrote magazine articles on weekends. I had sent one, cold, to a Catholic magazine that paid better than most, hoping it would be accepted. I got an editorial response that was both good and bad news, The editor liked my finely researched piece—about a program that was bringing black students from disadvantaged southern schools to spend their last two years of high school at Long Island institutions, living with volunteering families. The bad news was he wanted at least fifteen more photos and more quotes from the students themselves.

In order to comply, I had to reset interviews in four different towns and face another 150 miles of driving. Still, the money would pay one month's mortgage and so I said yes. The interviews were set up for a Saturday that turned out to be the coldest day of the year. I had to leave my children home alone, with the oldest ones in charge. As I drove away, I mentally rehearsed what each said they would do—Paul, a senior and the student government president, was working on an article for the school magazine; John, a sophomore, was doing an art project; Mary, in eighth grade, said she would do the ironing; Margee, nearly twelve, offered to make lunch; and nine-year-old Francis promised to play with Peter, four. I prayed to the Lord that nothing would mess up my idyllic image of loving siblings!

My work started with a complication. My camera attachment conked out right in the midst of my getting people ready for picture taking. I had to run around trying to find a camera store to replace my defective equipment. I finally found a new flash attachment, shelled out seventeen dollars, the sum total of cash I had on me, and got back to work.

I finished by 4 p.m., hungry from skipping lunch, tired, penniless on the road, and concerned about my kids back home. As I started to drive, I found myself getting colder and colder before I realized that the heater on my old Ford had broken. Somehow this was the final descent. My life, loaded with responsibilities since my teen years, started to hit me hard and all of a sudden I was shaking with sobs, trying to keep the car on the treacherous Long Island road. Who needs this life anyway? I shouted to no one listening. What was it all about—never stopping for a minute to rest, working day and night for six kids who would never know how much of my body and soul I had given to them? Life was just so much pain and discomfort and worry. At that moment, there was no Jesus there for me, as I truly wanted my frozen body to go numb and out—and never defrost again. I had never before felt such despair.

When I finally pulled into my driveway, I couldn't bend my fingers or feel my toes. I stumbled out of the car in the 5:30 pitch darkness, hoping my face didn't show the residue of tears.

My daughter Mary had run to the door and greeted me with a hug. I could sense her relief that I was safely home. She said immediately that she had water near boiling on the stove to make me some hot tea, and then I got an aroma of something delicious cooking in the oven. My thirteen-year-old Mary had made a meatloaf to surprise me. She had cleaned the house and kept the younger children peaceful. With these signs of love cloaking me so warmly, my low point of despair disappeared like melted ice.

I hugged my daughter, laughing, thanking her at first loudly, then silently. What a day it had been! On the one hand I had been dealing with strong negatives. But, like a sunburst, I had just seen the emergence of responsibility, consideration, love, and achievement above expectation in a daughter who was yet only on the brink of adolescence. How blessed I was. How joyful I felt. My daughter Mary had made me new, and had helped me remember that there is a road map to heaven, with only one sign pointing the way—Love.

Of course, I had always known this. I had given lessons on Jesus' road map for getting into heaven in Religion classes, underscoring how the Son of God had laid out the path so clearly. It was in Matthew 25, and it was beautiful—feed the hungry, give water to the thirsty, visit the prisoners, the sick, the abandoned ones. And where do we do this? On earth, right here. It was an amazing revelation, that heaven is right here, on this earth, and we're in this heaven, when we love others. And who must we love? Jesus told us. The poor, all of them, from all causes.

It's not a message we really want to hear, because the bottom line is that the road to heaven is blocked by the poor, and if we don't love them enough to help them, we can forget heaven. I have kept a book by a man named Chad Walsh from those days that well expresses how we turn away from following Jesus:

I know what I should do; there is nothing in the teachings of Christ that is clearer: go and love. But knowledge is one thing, deeds another. It seems as though I am two persons. One agrees with Christ and issues appropriate orders. The other, with his own peculiar serenity, plays deaf, and continues to live as though my ego were the central point of the cosmos and all galaxies revolved around it.

We not only play deaf, but add blindness, too. A real problem is that this blindness makes the poor invisible, and we like it that way. We can kid ourselves that we're heaven-bound if we don't "see" anybody who needs our help. You have to have a real experience of what it might feel like to be poor before you can have a valid empathy with the "outcasts" of our world. I remember a day when I learned this. I had been in New York City for a beautiful event, going to the Amato Opera to enjoy "The Marriage of Figaro." This was very special for me because my daughter Mary was singing the role of Cherubino. Everything was joyful until I had to return home to Connecticut where I live.

I was traveling by bus and had to go to the Port Authority on 8th Avenue. This was the first time in more than two years that I had been to that station. The last time I used this bus service, I was mugged, just across the street from the station. The thief nearly pulled my arm off in his determination to get my purse. Remembering this, I had come to the city without my purse, strapping a tiny bag around my waist for my car keys and a few dollars, covered over by my sweater. I didn't carry an overnight case. My belongings were in a plastic bag. I also wore old pants, flat shoes, and a twenty-year-old, getting shabby coat, described by my daughter Margee, a fashion designer, as a "got shabby" coat!

Clearly my motivation was to look poor so that I wouldn't be a target for a mugger or a panhandler. As I walked to the spot where my bus would leave, one of the homeless women referred to as "bag ladies" came up to me. She mumbled something, looked at the plastic bag I was carrying, and walked away. It occurred to me, somewhat embarrassingly, that she thought I was a bag lady, too.

Strange, but for a few minutes I felt a great identity with her. I was, in a sense, in disguise, to protect myself. But in so doing, I had become one of the anonymous, nameless people—like she was. I almost felt invisible, recalling the book by Ralph Ellison, written some four decades earlier about being black, an outcast of sorts in this society, which he titled *The Invisible Man*, and wrote:

"I am an invisible man. . . . I am a man of substance, of flesh and bone, fiber and liquids—and I might even be said to possess a mind. I am invisible, understand, simply because people refuse to see me."

When people don't want to associate with you because you are black, homeless, an addict, an ex-convict, and so on, they look past you and never see you. You are, then, invisible. Too often, the homeless and, yes, the poor—on a one-to-one encounter—are the invisible people. We can talk about them in categories, but we can't converse with them. We're afraid, because if we do, they may ask us to give something we don't want to give—our acknowledgment, perhaps, that they exist, and then, our help. This is exactly what Jesus wanted us to do, so definitively that he made our doing this a condition for entering heaven.

I had started that Sunday in my own familiar milieu. I ended it in an unfamiliar environment that, because of my mugging experience, I still perceived as hostile. But for a moment, I fit in when a bag lady thought I was one, like her. And what I learned was not comforting or consoling. I have been a Human Rights Commissioner, fought for civil rights, justice, equal opportunity, and have given money to the poor. I can feel good about all that. I can feel I'm doing my share to help the poor and the homeless.

But the truth is that I am part of the majority in our country who have a place to live, and an income—who move away from and pass by the invisible people when you can feel their breath. We just can't get that close. When Jesus said, "Feed the hungry," he meant that for every time and generation to come. But how close to them did he want us to get?

Perhaps as close as Mother Maria Skobtsova, a Russian Orthodox nun, would come to the starving, persecuted victims of war when, in her lifetime, war became a diabolical purge. As World War II began to rage out of control, she worked in France for the homeless, the hungry, the ill, many of them impoverished Russians who had come to France, seeking refuge from the German military assaults. When France was overtaken by the Nazis in 1940, she knew Paris had then become "a great prison." As she saw the increasing persecution of the Jews and the massive herding of Jewish men, women, and children being taken away to unknown fates, she, the priests, and good people she worked with tried to hide them, feed them, care for them, issuing baptismal certificates, as "proof" they were not Jewish, to try to save their lives.

In December 1942, as her work to aid the Jewish people became known to the Nazis in charge, Mother Maria and others who worked with her were deported to the Buchenwald concentration camp in Germany. She was sent a few months later, in a sealed cattle truck, to the Ravensbruck camp in Germany. She survived for two years, caring for others in the horrible camp, often giving her meager food to someone hungrier than herself. She was killed in a gas chamber in 1945. Her own words explain why she took what she believed is "the path to heaven:"

The way to God lies through love of people. At the Last Judgment I shall not be asked whether I was successful in my ascetic exercises, nor how many bows and prostrations I made. Instead I shall be asked, Did I feed the hungry, clothe the naked, visit the sick and the prisoners? That is all I shall be asked. About every poor, hungry, and imprisoned person the Savior says "I": "I was hungry, and thirsty, I was sick and in prison." To think that he puts *an equal sign* between himself and anyone in need. . . . I always knew it, but now it has somewhat penetrated to my sinews. It fills me with awe.

Thank God, for most of us, we don't have to endure the terminal suffering that some people, like Mother Maria, face if they say yes to traveling this road designed by Jesus. I, too, am awed, but my awe rises from meeting someone so connected to the Lord Jesus that she, like him, would give herself for others, to the death. Would I have the courage to follow Jesus' road map, as she did? In truth, I hope I am never tested to this degree, yet pray that I never misplace the road map written by Jesus.

I met Harvey Cox, the noted Protestant theologian, back in the 1960s and remember what he said: "We are now in a stage where we are so insulated from each other, from the hard facts of life, that unless you make intentional efforts to involve yourself and your children in the agony of humanity, it won't happen." That was nearly a half century ago, and we still have abundance that we don't share. Feeding the hungry is more complicated than it sounds, for it also means asking for a welfare set-up which aims not just at survival of the poor but also tries to maintain the dignity of those in need, and asking for the best foreign aid program to stem malnutrition in other nations. Can we understand that our abundance is also our education, our technical know-how, our agriculture, conservation, and planning expertise that should be shared with underdeveloped nations?

What was Jesus really telling us when he laid out the road map for getting to heaven? I think he was letting us know that we can't be his followers—Christians—on our own terms. Only when we respond to another person's needs do we make Christ present in the world, and if we don't do that, we can forget about heaven.

I made that point in a talk once to a church group and someone soundly challenged me. "Why the emphasis on the poor?" she complained. "Jesus had a good profession as a carpenter, and he enjoyed good meals with rich friends. It doesn't strike me that he was that poor."

Oh how clever we can be when we want to change the subject! I answered her, though I doubt what I said changed her set mind. When Jesus emphasized the poor, he wanted us to see that his Father had sent him to end the divisions, the separations among people, that have taken place on earth. He couldn't have made this clearer when he preached how we are all *one* with him and his Father. He told us to "Rejoice because your names are written in heaven," trying to make us see that there is no divisiveness among people in heaven. And he wanted us to know that heaven is not a destination, like New York or Chicago. Heaven is an oasis of love, where all are united to one another, where all barriers that separate us on earth—racial, national, cultural, economic, religious—are gone. Heaven is the radiant communion of saints, and there's only one road that gets us there, spelled out by Jesus—love.

He said, "Follow me," and affirmed, "By this shall all know that you are my followers, that you love one another as I have loved you." That's the road map, destination heaven.

3

Meeting—and *Re-Meeting—Jesus*

I looked for Christ in the hidden skies,

A flaming vision to blind my eyes—

While Christ walked by with stumbling feet

Along with the men of Madison Street.

—RAYMOND KRESENSKY

In 1950 I was a new mother of a feisty baby boy, Paul, living in a small town called Cape Vincent located at the edge of New York state where the St. Lawrence River and Lake Ontario seemed to meet. His father and I had moved to this village right after the wedding and we both taught school our first year there. Now, my husband was still teaching, but I was a stay-at-home mother, taking care of the apartment, cooking, cleaning, laundry, the usual. One thing that was different for me, a city girl, was that I had to walk to the post office every day to get the mail. They hadn't ever heard of "mail delivery" in that town where they used to say they did the census by watching to see if there were new diapers on a line. Then the population would go up by an additional "one," to add to the nearly nine hundred people living there.

Winters got very cold in this place they called "God's country," and the freezing temperatures began early. It was so cold one November day that year that I decided to stay home in the morning and bake a cake. It made sense to wait till afternoon to go out when, maybe, it would be a bit warmer. When I walked into the post office, I noticed a ragged-looking small boy, wearing a man's tattered jacket, standing by a wall. I ignored him for a few minutes, but then my curiosity took over, and I went over, wheeling Paul in the carriage, to talk to him.

First I asked him if he was cold. He said yes. Then I asked him if he was hungry. He said yes again. I asked him his name and he said Sterling. Then I said, "I just baked a cake. Would you like to come home with me and have cake and hot chocolate?" He smiled, and said, "Sure." I asked him a lot of questions as I served him and got some surprising answers, beginning with his age. I thought he was about eight years old. He was actually fifteen, and in high school. Oddly enough, he was rarely in town, almost never in the post office, and had gone in that afternoon only to try to warm his freezing body.

When my husband got home from school, we drove Sterling to the place where he lived. I was in shock to see poverty in this detail. He lived in a shack way out on an isolated farm, with no plumbing, no electricity, no intact walls, and trash strewn all over. I knew I had to look into why it was he lived here. I found he had a mother, who was on welfare, but his father had long been deceased. From time to time he had lived in foster homes. I wondered what kind of a difference it would make in his life if he were off welfare, had a decent place to live and a chance for a better education. Almost spontaneously, I asked him if he would like to come and live with us. He smiled and said yes. Within a few days, we met with his mother, who very nobly said that if he wanted to move in with us, she would agree. We informed the Welfare Department that Sterling was moving in with us and we would support him. They were delighted to have one less person getting their money.

In the next few months, we got to see what a great kid Sterling was, and home life was going well. Then we received the news that my husband was not going to have his contract renewed by the school. This meant he would have to get a job in some other area and we would have to move. At that point, I couldn't imagine sending Sterling back to where he'd come from. We had to adopt him, I insisted. I consulted with Father Reilly, the priest in town who had become our friend. He said he had only one concern, the closeness in our ages, since I was only twenty-two and Sterling was fifteen. However, since he knew about my young brothers and sisters and believed I thus had had much experience in the care of children, he wrote a very supporting letter. The adoption went through, and Sterling Bosco—he chose our name—was now our son.

Cape Vincent was a small town and one can imagine how the tongues wagged over this one. Why did the Boscos adopt a teenager? The only one who really knew was Father Reilly. I told him that I had not felt alone in the post office that afternoon. I truly felt Jesus was there, that he had arranged for me to come into the post office that afternoon, a very unusual time for me, precisely so I could see Sterling. The lines from Matthew 25 had gone through my head as I saw this child, hungry, cold, maybe homeless. I wanted to do what I believed Jesus would do. That's what I told Father Reilly, worrying that he might conclude that this twenty-two-year-old new mother was a delusional romantic. He didn't, at least not to my face. He took me at my word, said "God bless you," and wrote the deciding letter.

It turned out that Sterling had been baptized Catholic and had made his First Communion, thanks to a saintly woman who was his godmother. He and I have often felt that his deceased godmother, taking care of Sterling from her home in heaven, was in the post office that day, too. Father Reilly was having classes for an upcoming confirmation and let Sterling join in. By June, Sterling was confirmed, and we were packed, ready to move to Syracuse, New York. My husband had found another teaching job in a small town near that city.

Finding the right school for Sterling became a priority for me. We were now living in St. Lucy's parish, and I was happy to discover St. Lucy's parochial school included high-school as well as grammar school. Wondering how the nuns in charge would react when I told them I had a high-school age son, I went to the school to enroll Sterling. The nun in the office gave me a "you gotta be kidding" look, and told me I had to talk to the principal. Out walked the principal, tall and dignified. We looked at each other and fell into each other's arms. She was Sister Natalie, who had been my beloved senior English teacher at the Cathedral Academy in Albany! I felt assured that God was taking care of things and I knew immediately that all would be well. It was. Sterling graduated with honors, and then went into the Navy.

I could write a book about the joy Sterling—the son chosen some fifty years ago—has brought into my life. He's been a dedicated husband to his beautiful wife Bernadette; a devoted father of seven children, two of them adopted; a decorated police officer for the state of Illinois for nearly thirty years until a near fatal heart condition required his retirement; a fourth degree Knight of Columbus; a devoted parishioner of St. George Church in Tinley Park, Illinois, who worked with some other church members to turn an unused garage stall into a Perpetual Adoration Chapel; a grandfather of twelve beautiful children.

I met Jesus in the post office one cold November day in 1950, and have re-met him over and over ever since in all the people related to me because of Sterling. Their lives have touched mine because of that initial question I was moved to ask a ragged child, "Are you hungry?" Could I have ever imagined receiving an essay titled "A Woman of Character," with a first line saying, "My great grandmother, Antoinette Bosco, is a very incredible person, as well as an award-winning author. When I get older, I want to be just like her." I was so honored that young Amy Miller, daughter of my granddaughter Bonnie, daughter of my son Sterling, wrote that. Humbly I was reminded that God challenges us—and rewards us—in ways we ourselves could never design.

First, of course, we have to recognize that there is a challenge and that it is coming from God. I was put on alert about this a long time ago when I happened to read a story written by Leo Tolstoy, called "Where Love Is, There God Is Also." I was always reading, drawn especially to anything in print that had to do with religion or spirituality. With a title like that one, I got to reading this right away.

This is a simple story, with one main character, a shoemaker who works in a basement. There is only one window, but he looks through this to stay in touch with the outside world, even though all he really sees are the shoes and boots of the people passing. He is a religious man, who often reads the New Testament. One night, reading the story of the rich man who invites Jesus to dinner, not really recognizing who he is, the shoemaker begins to wonder about himself. If Christ were to visit him one day, would he recognize who he is?

Later that night he has a dream in which he hears a voice telling him, "Look tomorrow on the street. I am coming." In the morning he keeps thinking of that mysterious voice, and goes to the window to peer up so he can see not just the feet, but the faces of the people passing. The first person he sees is an old soldier, wearily shoveling snow. He is moved and impulsively invites him in for hot tea. As they talk, the subject turns to Christ and his love for the poor and the sinful.

After the tattered soldier leaves, the shoemaker, peering out the window, sees a woman with no coat or warm clothing holding a crying baby. He quickly tells them to come in, and then he gives some warm food to the mother, while he holds and plays with the baby. As she goes to leave, he gives her a coat and some money.

Later he hears a slight commotion outside and going to his window he sees an old woman who sells apples holding onto a poor boy who tried to steal one of them. Concerned that the woman would bring the boy to the police, who would soundly whip him, the shoemaker runs out to try to make peace between them. The boy, contrite, offers to help the woman by carrying her bag, and the two of them walk off tranquilly together.

That evening, the old shoemaker picks up his Bible as always, but suddenly remembers his dream. At the same time, he hears sounds. He looks around and discerns figures in the dark corner of his room. "It was I," someone says. It was the old soldier, who then disappears. "And it was I," the same voice says, coming from the woman with her baby. She vanishes, the apple woman and the boy appear and the voice continues "It was I," as they, too, leave.

Now the Bible opens, as if on its own, to the page where he reads, "For I was hungered, and you gave me meat: I was thirsty, and you gave me drink: I was a stranger, and you took me in." He reads further down, "Inasmuch as you have done it to the least of these, you have done it to me." Then it was that the shoemaker knew without a doubt who it was that had visited him three times that day.

I loved that Tolstoy story for what I learned from it at a very young age, that if someone needs something essential to maintain body and soul, it is not their need alone. It is Christ's need, too. If a child is hungry, it is the Christ-child who is hungry. Yet, if someone gives the food to nourish the hungry, it is Christ who is serving. The suffering Christ and the serving Christ are one and the same. We meet and re-meet Christ everywhere we turn. But, the challenge is—do we recognize him, or do we only see a soldier, a mother and baby, an old woman and a boy?

But now comes the confusion. We meet so many people in the course of our lives who are mean, selfish, disgusting, unfair, and descriptive of all the terrible capital sins. How many stories can each of us tell about people who have hurt us, who have no compassion, no concern for others, who without conscience steal from them, everything from money to their lives? How do we meet Christ in them?

I remember so many encounters with mirror-opposites of Jesus in my lifetime. Back in the late 1960s, I was a reporter with *The Long Island Catholic*, a job I loved. But there was a huge problem. Money. I was then divorced, raising and supporting my six birth children entirely on my own, without a penny coming in from any source other than my own earnings. The paper couldn't afford to give me the salary I needed to make ends meet. I started looking at the want ads and saw one that excited me. It was for a job with a newspaper that seemed to fit me to a T, and the salary was once and a half what I was earning. Best of all, it was being offered by a woman's employment agency. How fortunate! There would be a woman in charge who would really understand my predicament and my family's needs.

I made an appointment and filled out the necessary forms. Then I got in to talk to the woman who owned the agency. She looked at everything I wrote, nodding, until she came to the last line. There the question was asked about children. Being honest, I had written in that

I had six. She glared at me first, then asked how much money my husband made. I told her I had no husband, that I was a divorced, single mother. It was then she actually raised her voice in anger.

"Why are you wasting my time?" she yelled. "I would never send you any place for an interview. If one of your children got sick, you'd stay out of work. You'd be the most undependable employee they'd ever have."

I asked her if she'd say that to a man. She answered, "Of course not,'" going on about how for a man the job would come first and he'd have his wife home to take care of the children.

Well, that was 1968 and times were different then for working women. But what I never forgot was her meanness. I remember my anger, followed by my prayers, asking the Lord, rather automatically, to forgive me. I challenged Jesus, asking him how I was going to see anything of him in her. I don't know how long it took me to discover what Jesus wanted me to learn from this bad encounter, but learn it I did, and it came from an unexpected source.

I had come across something written back in the thirteenth century by the German mystic, Meister Eckhart, and it startled me. "A man has many skins in himself, covering the depths of his heart. Man knows so many other things; he does not know himself. Why, thirty or forty skins or hides, just like an ox's or bear's, so thick and hard, cover the soul. Go into your own ground and learn to know yourself."

I thought I knew myself quite well, but I was getting a message that maybe I had to do more very important self-learning, beginning by focusing on my anger. Why had that woman stirred this rage in me? As I simmered down, I could face the truth and honestly admit that I was insulted; my ego had been tampered with. Nothing she said made me a less competent writer or less of a good mother. No, all she had messed with was my image of myself. Now I knew where to go, straight to Jesus. He told me to straighten out. Soften your heart and forgive her. Then you'll know who you are.

So now I started to focus on understanding exactly how Jesus is present in everyone, even the cruel, miserable, unattractive ones. Before long, it became clear to me that this experience was all about me finding him in myself, not in the other person. He was helping me see that when we have to deal with people who seem to bear no resemblance to him, he is there, *with us*. Even Oscar Wilde, the brilliant, troubled writer, learned this. He wrote, "When Christ says 'Forgive your enemies,' it is not for the sake of the enemy, but for one's own sake that he says so, and because love is more beautiful than hate. In his own entreaty to the young man, 'Sell all that thou hast and give to the poor,' it is not of the state of the poor that he is thinking, but of the soul of the young man, the soul that wealth was marring."

I thought studying and praying would bring me the consolation of feeling closer to Jesus, and it did, but not in the way I expected. It brought me to a fearful admission that I, too, would always be in need of forgiveness, and that I would be meeting Jesus many times in my life in all those who would forgive me for whatever I did that might hurt them. I found help in the writings of wise ones, like American theologian Reinhold Niebuhr, who wrote: "Forgiving love is a possibility only for those . . . who feel themselves in need of divine mercy, who live in a dimension deeper and higher than that of moral idealism, feel themselves as well as their fellow men convicted of sin by a holy God and know that the differences between the good man and the bad man are insignificant in his sight. . . . For this reason the religious ideal of forgiveness is more profound and more difficult than the rational virtue of tolerance."

It took a while, but eventually I could acknowledge that in the employment office with that miserable woman, I had re-met Jesus.

Other times there was no confusion at all about who I was meeting. The day I interviewed Gertrude Unger, then a retired New York City schools administrator and textbook author, I left her home soaring. She was a lovely, quiet woman, devoted to the Lord. I was entranced by the peacefulness of her presence, and though I was interviewing her on a number of educational issues, I knew there was something deeper in her. I wanted to know what that was. So out of the blue, I stopped, looked intensely at her and asked honestly, "Why are you different?"

I took her off guard, and she was silent for a moment. Then, with tears in her eyes, she said quietly, fingering a crucifix on a chain around her neck, "When I was young, I used to think that all that was important was my brilliance, my achievements as an educator and a writer. But now I know that only one thing is important—goodness."

She gave me no life story of difficult times or personal pains. She only told me truth, what she had learned from her life, and it was the truth of Jesus. I left her that day, but never forgot her. I knew that now I could better understand the effect Jesus had on the people he met in his lifetime on this earth. He must have made them want to ask the same question of him, "Why are you different?"

Jesus continually surprises us in the ways he shows up so we can meet him again and again. I remember having the unexpected pleasure of encountering a woman who reminded me of the need we have to care for and help one another—especially the homeless. I think I would have loved to have tea and conversation with her if she were still around, but as it happens, she died nearly 140 years ago.

The meeting between us came about because I have a passion. I'm crazy about books and where they take me—always into a new world of ideas, information, the human condition, beauty, humor, what have you. On this day I had been driving through a small town in Vermont when I saw a sign, "Library Book Sale." Naturally, I came to an immediate halt. I picked up many books, but one that really caught my eye was an old book of poetry with its once elegant cover taped on. It was written by a woman named Adelaide Proctor who died in 1864 at the age of thirty-nine.

What first caught my eye as I opened this very tattered book was the introduction. It was written by Charles Dickens. He told how he, as the editor of a weekly journal called "Household Words," had published some of her work and had come to know her and her family well. His admiration for her went far beyond her proficiency as a poet. She was a true, caring, outgoing worker for others, he said. Converted to the Roman Catholic faith at age twenty-seven, Miss Proctor "devoted herself to a variety of benevolent objects," he wrote.

"Now it was the visitation of the sick that had possession of her; now it was the sheltering of the houseless; now it was the elementary teaching of the densely ignorant . . . now it was the wider employment of her own sex in the general business of life; now it was all these things at once. Perfectly unselfish, swift to sympathize and eager to relieve, she wrought at such designs with a flushed eagerness that disregarded season, weather, time of day or night, food, rest," wrote Mr. Dickens of this remarkable woman.

From her writings, it is clear that she was consumed with empathy for those, particularly women and children, who had no shelter in her country of England in the mid-1800s, "women and children utterly forlorn and helpless, either wandering about all night, or crouching under a miserable archway. . . . It is a marvel that we could sleep in peace in our warm, comfortable homes with this horror at our very door," she wrote.

As I read her poems, I felt some of them had such a universal timeliness they could have been written today, like one she called "Homeless:"

> Look out at the farthest corner
> Where the wall stands blank and bare:
> Can that be a pack which a Peddler
> Has left and forgotten there?
> His goods lying out unsheltered
> Will be spoilt by the damp night air.
>
> Nay; goods in our thrifty England
> Are not left to lie and grow rotten,
> For each man knows that market value
> Of silk or woolen or cotton.
> But in counting the riches of England
> I think our poor are forgotten.

It didn't matter that I never got to have tea with Adelaide Procter, because I knew her well. Her name was Jesus and I loved her.

The actual truth is that we can't avoid meeting and re-meeting Jesus, even though not everyone gets to know this. A half a century ago writer Chad Walsh proclaimed, "To find Christ, you do not need to leave your block; you do not need to leave your house. Where the needs of food and drink and clothing and medicine do not exist, there are other needs as imperious: a child wishing to learn the alphabet, a wife with more dishes than she can conveniently do, a friend whose need is simply, but desperately for someone with patience, sympathy and listening ears . . . The face of Christ is likely to be most clearly visible when one is ministering to the bluntest needs."

What I learned in the next few years is that working for *The Long Island Catholic*, even for low pay, was the place where, I truly believe, Jesus wanted me to be. Meeting Sister Thelma Hall, a Cenacle sister, at their convent and on Long Island, proved that for me.

I used to make retreats there, and occasionally, as a reporter for the diocesan Catholic paper, I would do a story about something newsworthy going on here. The Cenacle sisters had a mission, "to awaken and deepen faith" by providing a space for spiritual growth through prayer, contemplation, guided retreats, and reflective programs adapted to the needs of people. One day when I had gone there just to pray and meditate, I met Sister Thelma Hall, and found a friend I would forever cherish.

Sister Thelma told me that the work of the Cenacle was to reach people not reached by the traditional avenues offered by church programs. She asked me if I could think of a group needing to be noticed. This was spring, 1970, and by then, I had been a single mother for nearly four years, raising and financially supporting my six birth children. Sterling, much older, was now married and a father himself. I think it took me about two seconds to respond to Sister Thelma. A group needing to be noticed? Indeed, "divorced and separated Catholics," I responded, telling her I was one of those "forgotten people" and we desperately wanted the church to recognize us.

Sister Thelma, a convert who, because of her own faith search, had a tremendous empathy for others, jumped on this. We immediately began to work together to get diocesan approval to call a first-ever meeting for divorced and separated Catholics. That wasn't easy, especially when I was asked by a priest in the Chancery

Office if this would be for women only. "Of course not," I answered. With a very concerned look on his face, he said, "That wouldn't be right to invite men. Don't you realize that some of them might want to start dating?" "Father," I said, patiently, "don't you realize that they might be already dating?" His face got red, but he gave us permission to invite both men and women.

We advertised the meeting in the *Pennysaver*. All divorced and separated Catholics were invited to come to the Cenacle on a Sunday afternoon and feel again their connection with the church. To our amazement, hundreds showed up. We ran these programs for years, and if "imitation is the finest form of flattery," we were flattered. The ministry for divorced and separated Catholics was picked up, first by the Paulists in Boston, and then in various places around the country.

Ten years later, I was invited by Father Dennis Regan, then the rector of the major seminary on Long Island, to speak before some 120 Bishops on "Spirituality for the Divorced and Separated." I thought there might be a quiet, polite applause at the end of my talk. No. The Bishops gave me a standing ovation and several told me afterwards that they would go back to their dioceses and start to begin the healing needed after so long ignoring the divorced and separated in their flocks.

I even got a very warm and personal congratulations for my courage to speak out from a remarkable man who was there, Cardinal Leon-Joseph Suenens. A few years later, I received a handwritten note from this God-centered man, "May the Lord be your strength in daily life and your joy forever. I send you a little booklet for Easter reading. With my cordial blessings, L.J. Cardinal Suenens." I'll cherish this correspondence forever that came from a man who radiated Jesus in his presence and his words, notably when he said, "My hope is that we are moving towards a church that is closer to

Pentecost than to canon law." One was re-meeting Jesus when Cardinal Suenens was there, for as Jesuit theologian Father Walter Burghardt said, "He is a cardinal, yes. But he has transformed the meaning of cardinal from 'prince of the church' to 'servant of man.'"

I stayed in touch with Sister Thelma Hall over the years, learning from her wisdom which always poured out like healing balm, blended with compassion, humanity, openness, and humor. You could never doubt that Jesus was present when she was around. When Sister Thelma died in October 2002, our mutual friend Karen Musicaro sent me an e-mail with her memories at the memorial services for this cherished woman. "She is remembered as the musician, the artist, the poet, the writer, the friend, the challenger, the maverick, the mystic who is, of course, better known as 'the lover.' Each testimony of her love, her feisty spirit, her idiosyncratic ways, her tenderness, her bluntness, her obstinate determination filled the room with tears, with laughter and with Thelma." I was struck with how this sounded like a mini-biography of Jesus.

I had to learn that Jesus' ways may be different from ours, but they are always better. I would have left that job with *The Long Island Catholic* if I had been offered employment elsewhere. But then, I never would have met Sister Thelma to begin the work that brought Jesus' love to us forgotten ones in a way he would have wanted, through his church.

When the time was right, I did get an unexpected job offer. I had written a story for *The Long Island Catholic* about a new venture beginning at the State University of New York at Stony Brook, the development of a Health Sciences Center, which would have six schools, including a medical school, and a University hospital. I had done a one-on-one interview with Dr. Edmund Pellegrino who was hired to be the organizer. After the story ran, he called me to say I was the only one who really understood the very human, as well as professional, innovations he planned to bring to this Center. I had gleaned his spiritual motivations, verified for me when I learned how devoted this father of seven was to his Catholic faith, and this had, perhaps, subtly flavored my story. Not long after, at Dr. Pellegrino's invitation, I was offered a position to design and head up a community relations department for the Health Sciences Center, at a significant increase in salary from what I had been earning.

It had become clear to me by this time in my life that we do indeed re-meet Jesus over and over, but it's on a scale of importance and wonderment not designed by us. I have seen Jesus at the checkout counter in a supermarket, in a co-worker who brought me a cup of water, in a friend who called just to say "how are you." But I had to learn that meeting Jesus in life-changing ways always happens on his schedule, not ours.

I look at him, still beckoning to me, and I repeat words said long ago which so often have well applied to my life—"The good wine you have saved till now."

4

The Jesus Who *Understood Human Pain*

Show me what kind of God you have
and I will tell you what kind of
humanity you possess.

—EMIL BRUNNER

I remember that morning in August of 1993 so vividly. My radio alarm had awakened me with the playing of one of my late son Peter's favorite pieces of music. I fell apart. Crying hysterically, I looked at the high school graduation photos of my seven children on the wall next to my bed. How often had I laughed and joked that there was my life on that wall! But this morning all I could see were the two who were gone, Peter and John, both from a bullet in their heads.

In my pain I told myself, I can't get up, emphasis on *can't*. But somewhere from far away I remembered reading a line that said, "If you think you can't, you're right." It shook me. I knew that if I didn't get up that morning, I'd be stuck in my pain and I'd be lost.

I cried out to Jesus to help me, looking at my picture of him that I had mounted on the wall next to my bed in every bedroom I had slept in for exactly fifty years to the month. My attention became riveted as I stared, for, with the sun streaming into the room, it seemed as if the figure of Jesus, which had always been an embossed one, was almost emerging from the flat, framed background. The light from the window was actually focusing on the heart of Jesus. I stood, looking at Jesus' image again, as I had nearly every day for fifty years, and felt the words, "Look at my heart." I had usually focused on his beckoning fingers, but now I stared, seeing as if for the first time that his heart was pierced, encircled with his crown of thorns, with his cross implanted in his heart.

I understood what Jesus wanted me to grasp, that he was one with me in my pain, that his heart was as mutilated as mine. He wanted me to feel his compassion, and let me know that he understood all the emotions I was going through. He wanted to assure me that he would never leave me orphaned. I remembered how often in his public ministry he had understood human pain, how he had constantly healed the sick, like the paralytic, the lepers, the centurion's servant, Peter's mother-in-law, the blind ones, the bleeding woman, and even raised the daughter of a synagogue leader from the dead, as well as bringing life back to his friend Lazarus. I couldn't ask him to bring back my dead sons, but I was aware that he knew I needed the healing. More than that, I trusted he would restore me to a wholeness if I trusted him. I looked at his heart, which was my heart—and chose that morning to live.

I wasn't in an easy place either emotionally or spiritually. I was still mourning terribly the suicide of my youngest son Peter, who at age twenty-seven had ended his earthly life on March 18, 1991. And now I had been hit with another devastating tragedy. The day before that August 1993 morning when I didn't ever want to get out of bed, I had gotten the horrendous news from a sheriff in Montana that my son John and his wife Nancy had been found murdered, shot to death in the middle of the night as they slept in the bedroom of their newly purchased home. My life would be forever reshaped, and the cross would be imbedded in my heart till my last breath, but I wasn't lost. I had been put unwillingly on the path of pain that had been pioneered before me by the very Son of God. He understood, and he loved me. That was the message. I believed that morning that I could now go forward in hope, holding the hands of my living children and my big family, the hands of Jesus.

In the years since Peter's death, I have talked and met with so many parents who have suffered this tormenting tragedy, as I have. Always, I feel more fortunate than most of them, for I had help from an unexpected source, Peter himself. My son had left us individual notes, and a very long tape, hoping to help explain why, with so much going for him, he had made that choice which would leave all his loved ones in so much pain. Considering his accomplishments—he had served two years in the U.S. Army, graduated from college, was a brilliant educator who had taught math in a Catholic school in Guam, and had already written three war-history books—we were beyond baffled.

The dominating theme in the notes and tape he left was a contradiction. It seemed that Peter had not really chosen death. He wanted a new life. Certainly one sign of that was evident in retrospect on Palm Sunday, one week before he left us. During that week he kept passing out Easter eggs to everyone, and the symbolism was clear to him, if not to us, at the time. In fact, a letter sent to a Japanese friend of his that he left on the computer indicated this. He said, "Soon it will be our holiday of Easter. At this time of year we give our friends eggs and bunny rabbits made of candy. They symbolize the fertility and rebirth of the earth in spring."

Then, too, Peter and I had often talked in the past years of how this life is but a prelude to a fuller existence. We quoted C. S. Lewis who said we live here on earth in a "shadowland," for "This is not our permanent home." In the note he left me Peter wrote that for him, it was "time to go home." That being said, I could be happy he wanted to be with Jesus in heaven, but it did not ease the tormenting question of why he put a bullet to his head.

Strangely enough, I think that question tormented Peter, too. In the tape he left, he tells us at the outset that his death, like his life, is an enigma, to himself as well as to others. Yet, what comes through is his tormenting struggle when he came to believe he was not fully equipped to be able to handle life as it is required to be lived on this earth, particularly his inability to accept the cruelty that had come down through the centuries that he often referred to as "man's inhumanity to man." He had what he called "a missing part," explaining that something in the deep down, crucial, essential mechanism that one needs to be able to greet—and not just endure—each day was missing. He said he had everything, good health, good looks, good education, great family; "My life is like a Rolls Royce without sparkplugs. It looks great, but it has a hidden flaw that keeps it from running properly. The absence of that spark has often made even the simplest setbacks for me almost unendurable."

Because he was so sensitive and brilliant, he knew he was "flawed," as he put it, and thus unable to fully participate in the connections to people and the world that are essential to humans. He so often said he was doomed to be lonely and, God knows, that's about the worst state a human being can endure. We can take physical pain, setbacks, cruelty against us, even loss—almost anything—so long as we still connect with others. But for the person who can't connect, not really, because the part that is essential to making that connection is missing—that person is truly doomed to a terminal hell on earth. And that was Peter's pain.

And yet, we, his family and friends, didn't have a clue that he was moving permanently away from us. How could we? He was so vital, so interested in so many things, so much fun, and we loved him in such a special way.

Only a few days before he left us I was teasing him about how when he was a baby, we called him our "Focolare." I had done a story back in the 1960s about the Focolare Movement in the Catholic Church. Focolare means fireplace in Italian, and the idea of this movement was to find a center, like a fireplace, where there would be light and love and warmth, a center to remind us of God.

Well, Peter certainly was our Focolare. Born when the other five ranged in age from five to thirteen, he was the focus where we could spill out our love on the innocent child. He refreshed us. The other five could have their sibling encounters, but disruption couldn't remain in the atmosphere of our home because we had this beautiful child here. He drew out the love each of us had inside us. That's what Peter was to us, our family center, our focus of love, and, oh yes, our entertainment, too. He was very funny in so many delightful ways.

We never mourned for Peter. We celebrated his life. That's what he wanted. In the note he left me, he said:

> Do not arrange a funeral. Let there instead be a simple, intimate gathering of friends and family. Ask that no black garments be worn, but rather, bright, spring clothing. Prepare a hearty meal for the occasion. Let this gathering be not a time of mourning, but a time of healing. Lay my spirit to rest. For by accepting my death, you will affirm life.

Feel no guilt, for there is no fault. Weep not for me. For mine was a pleasant and joyful life. Having cherished my time on earth, I now embrace death, just a man may relish his two-weeks vacation, yet be glad to be back home.

Be happy for your son. For like a wave closing on a drowning man, my suffering is ended. Know that I loved you dearly.

These are my wishes.

His time on earth was brief, but how blessed we were to have had that shining moment with Peter. Of course, it has remained impossible for me not to weep. No mother buries a child, of any age, without being completely and permanently altered. I put my fate into Jesus' hands over and over, always begging him to take care of Peter for me. Then came a night when I was given an incredible gift. As I spoke to Jesus, he showed me where Peter was, on a beach, with him, and the two of them, enjoying the rhythmic motion of the waves, were laughing.

Some might say I imagined this. That would get me laughing. I learned at a very young age, when I was six or seven, that heaven is very much in touch with earth, and that "e vero" came from my good Italian grandmother, who was extremely devoted to St. Joseph, I know not why. Many years earlier, when she and my grandfather had come to this country, settling in Rome, New York, they had bought a house and set up a little grocery store on the first floor. She loved to tell us what came next. One day a very poor man, with a beard, came in. He was hungry and he wanted to buy some food, but he had no money. Something about him touched her, and even though she was poor, too, she gave him food and waved him on. He smiled and that's when she saw who he was. St. Joseph! I never doubted that she was right, after all, she was my grandmother. Years later, when I heard of Dorothy Day saying always be good to someone in need because, who knows, "you might be entertaining angels," I thought of my grandmother and thanked her for the faith she passed on to us!

Why should we ever doubt the reality of communication between the two worlds of earth and heaven? My writer friend, Mitch Finley, a few years back put an ad in newspapers asking for true stories of people who had experienced the presence of deceased loved ones. He was showered with responses, and in the book he then wrote, *Whispers of Hope,* he related "contact" experiences as told even by such respected people as Thomas Merton, Frederick Buechner, and C. S. Lewis. I can personally attest, many times over, to the truth of such encounters. Human pain is well understood by the Lord who would give relief to all who are so badly burdened.

After Peter died, a literary agent I knew, Henry Morrison, gave me a book he thought I'd find comforting. It had been written by David Morrell, author of *First Blood,* the novel on which the Rambo movies were based. It was titled *Fireflies,* and was his personal story of his agony over watching his fifteen-year-old son, Matthew, suffer and die from bone cancer. He wrote of having experienced several "mystical" events after Matthew died, one of them, fireflies. I gasped, remembering the night, shortly after Peter's death, when I stood at my bedroom window, empty and agonized. Suddenly, there were fireflies, so many of them, sending out blue, red, and silver sparks. I felt a rush of heat descending from my head to my feet, and all I could say was "Peter!" I didn't tell anybody. I didn't want anybody to think I was losing it!

But now I was reading David Morrell's experience, as he was hunching over a bed, sobbing. I knew that position. It was mine, too. Then suddenly, he writes, "Fireflies filled the dark bedroom . . . these lights zigged and darted, zagged and swirled . . . the room was ablaze with them. . . . Fireflies. Splendrous! Of varying colors but all of equal magnificence." He felt that one of them was the spirit of his son, with a message: "Dad, I want to play . . . I don't hurt any more, I'm at peace. I'm where I belong."

Two grieving parents, in two different parts of the country, in two different years, but both receiving the strange gift of fireflies. David Morrell's book was an affirmation for me of the mysterious ways we are linked to heaven, and how more fitting could it be than getting the heavenly gift of sparkling lights—to light up our darkness.

After John died, it was the music that would bring on the tears, and the smile. I had taken him to a concert when he was seven and, for him, it was love at first sound for the violin. He played the violin well enough to be in the second section of a concert put on by a symphony orchestra in Boulder, Colorado, where he had set up a furniture making business a decade earlier. I was in the audience, bursting with pride. One of the works they played was Tchaikovsky's Waltz from Eugene Onegin. I was in my car a few days after I got the news of his death by murder and I was crying, calling out to Jesus to let me know if my John was at peace. At that moment, music burst out from my car radio. It was the Waltz from Eugene Onegin. Funny thing is, I hadn't turned the radio on!

John had lived out west for twenty years, but a few thousand miles had never kept us apart. Besides frequent phone calls, I would fly out to Colorado, where he had moved out of love for nature, especially the Rocky Mountains. I remember one visit in particular where we had the chance to spend two full days together. John and I drank pots of coffee, talked late into the night about days gone by, about how he always helped someone in need, even, literally, once giving a homeless man the shirt off his back. We drove together in his then seven-year-old van to Flagstaff Mountain, over some homemade roads that led to a thirty-five-acre paradise, listened to water moving in a creek, absorbed the vision of trees and rock formations, gazed over a city, and silently praised the Creator.

We went to his shop and I saw the wood and machines my son, an artist with wood, manipulated into beautiful furniture. He showed me some samples of examples of exotic woods he had bought, simply for their beauty. He was awed by the hand of the Creator who had put such hidden, Divine artistry into wood. I remembered when he was no more than seven or eight, how he devised his own form of art, building intricate structures with toothpicks and glue. I had marveled at such early signs of creative talent.

The richness of this visit was vast, made more so by the memories of all we had shared from his beginnings within me. I looked at his strong, muscular body and remembered the infant, six weeks old, ill with a pneumonia that would not respond to medication. I had watched him shrink back to his birth weight, and prayed. For the two days that his illness was called critical, I made my private bargain with God, pledging to accept any pain he asked, if he would keep my baby alive.

During those two days of exclusive time with John, an incident at a supermarket communicated to me the kind of person he had become. We passed a child sitting in a grocery cart. John smiled at him, talked to him. The child laughed out loud with pleasure at this unexpected attention from a man. "Children," John commented, "are very important persons. What a shame that too many adults treat them like little annoying things." That didn't sound too original to me. I think John had heard that from a friend named Jesus.

In the morning John had to take me to the airport. He had the coffee ready, and he was dressed, not in his work clothes, but in his very best suit. "John, why?" I asked, knowing he would have to change into work clothes when he got home. His mother was special, he said, his best friend, and he had dressed in the appropriate way to show this.

I thought I could never be more touched again, but I was, not too long before John was killed, when he sent me a letter, mentioning so many of his good friends. His last paragraph said, "Most of all I thank God for my closest friend, confidant and supporter, my mother. If good luck could be measured, there still would be no measure adequate to reflect the blessing you have been in my life. When I begin to falter or doubt myself, I look at all you've done for me, and my strength returns. I know I am worth it, whatever the effort, because I can see in you the reflection of the principles you've taught me in the person you've become. I love and admire that person. Love always, John."

Could any mother ever have received a gift more beautiful than that?

My children and I now all cherish some of the beautiful furniture my carpenter son made. Shortly after his death I came across a poem titled "Jesus the Carpenter," written by man named Charles M. Sheldon, that so well expresses our devotion to the beauty John left us:

> If I could have the table Christ
>
> Once made in Nazareth,
>
> Not all the pearls in all the sea,
>
> Nor crowns of kings or kings to be
>
> As long as men have breath,
>
> Could buy that thing of wood he made—
>
> The Lord of Lords who learned a trade.

Just having the tables, the bookcases, the cabinets John made is so much more than a legacy. They are the last of their kind, precious, a perpetual benediction in our homes.

More joy came to our family when John met Nancy. They were married only two years when they decided to move to Montana, and were murdered a few months later by the eighteen-year-old son of the people from whom they had purchased a home. I had visited them in Boulder a few months earlier and Nancy had shared her journal with me, showing me poems and writings expressing her values and philosophies. We laughed a bit about how "homespun" her beliefs were. She was, after all, a South Dakota farm girl. A week before her death, she had been making raspberry jam for Christmas presents with a neighbor. Her journal was in the kitchen.

So many of her entries were about the wonder, the blessing, the necessity of love. She starred some words of Thornton Wilder that I felt were inspired by Jesus: "Love will have been enough; all those impulses of love return to the Love that made them."

I read these words as my sons Paul, Frank, and I packed John and Nancy's belongings in that Montana house with its blood-soaked bedroom.

Funny how people tell you "you'll get over it," trying to comfort you in your pain from the loss of children, not understanding that this is a terminal pain. Only one could understand this, the one who suffers with us, because he made us. I kept getting closer and closer to Jesus, as I felt him drawn to me like a magnet force. There was a reason for this and I found it unexpectedly—or was it?—in a book that fell into my hands on the revelations of Julian of Norwich. Father John Swanson, an Episcopal priest, was clarifying Julian's words. He writes:

If one reads Julian carefully, one discovers that she does not say that Christ is like our mother—but rather differently, that it is Christ whom our mothers are like. In fact, it is within the Christ that we find the "feminine" love which we then see reflected in the love of a mother for her child. It is not that Christ's love is like a mother's love; it is rather that the source and origin of mother-love is Christ. Our mothers love us with Christ's love. To be a loving mother is to be Christ.

It had been hard for me to really see that my pain was Jesus' pain. Now I could better understand why he wanted me to see his heart speared with the cross. But I could also understand why he wanted me to remember all the goodness and joy my sons had brought into my life. That was his memory, too.

5

The Jesus Who Works in

Mysterious Ways to Reach Us

*Look, here you can see how our Lord
calls you and all others who are willing
to listen to him.*

—WALTER HILTON

The summer after Peter died I was rearranging
books on a shelf when I came across one I had
read fifteen years earlier that had become a
best seller. It was *Life After Life* by Dr.
Raymond Moody, the first of the many-to-come books
on "near death experiences." As I often do, I began
reading segments of it again, quickly caught by a
question and answer segment, where this was asked:
"Have you ever interviewed anyone who has had a
near-death experience in association with a suicide
attempt? If so, was the experience any different?"

The answer distressed me. Yes, he wrote, experiences
from attempted suicide were an "unpleasant, limbo

state" where they were led to believe suicide was an unfortunate act which could be "attended with a severe penalty."

Perhaps it was the journalist in me, though more likely the mother, but I wanted to know firsthand what Dr. Moody meant by that. I felt I had been given many signs that Peter was "home," joyfully with Jesus. It took me a few months to get up some courage, but that fall of 1991, I did something really out of character for me. I had seen where Dr. Moody was to be a main presenter at a conference in Baltimore. I signed up and went there, hoping to meet him.

As it turned out, that didn't happen, but what I did learn was that this fine man was launching a new research project on how some people have visionary encounters with departed loved ones. He was inviting people who might be good subjects for this to get in touch with him. I responded immediately, calling Dr. Moody at his home in Alabama. I told him it was very important to me that I come and have a professional visit with him, for which I would gladly pay him. To my surprise, he was utterly human and friendly, said we could discuss payment later, and apologized that there would be a delay in getting together. He told me he had a bad thyroid problem which would have him hospitalized for a while, and invited me to come in January when he would be recuperating.

It took two plane rides and a car trip to find his isolated house, an old grist mill on the banks of a stream, but within five minutes of being with this man, I felt at home. I told him I had come because my son Peter had committed suicide and I was distressed over what he wrote in his book about the near death experiences of those who had attempted suicide. I wanted to know what he really believed about death after suicide. Immediately, he leaned toward me, assuring me that he had interviewed many who had attempted suicide and then had had beautiful, comforting experiences. He said he had put that suicide question in his book to please his editors. I took a deep breath and thanked him.

I was the only one there with him early that morning, and it was an encounter never to be forgotten in how our conversation turned immediately to faith. He told me he had had a kind of neardeath experience himself, in which he saw Christ and with Christ reviewed his whole life. We found we were both in agreement on how, at this point in our lives, the only thing that brought excitement or interest was the spiritual search. Most everything else had a boredom factor.

At this point a visitor came in. Dr. Moody introduced me to Dannion Brinkley, a man who had had two profound near death experiences and had come out of these with amazing psychic gifts. They were researching new possibilities for healing to come from the near death experience. At this time Dannion was not well known. He had not yet completed his book, *Saved by the Light*, later made into a movie starring Eric Roberts, brother of actress Julia Roberts.

Dr. Moody introduced me, saying simply, "Toni is here to talk to me because her son Peter, who was sensitive and loved and not on drugs, committed suicide." I kept making it clear that it struck me I had really come here hoping to find some direction and maybe some answers to the question which had plagued me for the past ten months, "What am I to learn from Peter's death?" I spent the day there, with those two very spiritual men, learning so much about their lives and their work, participating in their research. But it was Dannion's vision about Peter that most affected me.

He said that Peter's death was definitely because of a past life experience that had prevented him from doing the special work he was supposed to do in this life. As Dannion explained it, Peter was born to be of "the priesthood of Jesus," some specific "Order" that was unknown to me. He said Peter's work, like that of Jesus', was to start in his twenty-eighth year, when he would begin a new cycle. But, sadly, Peter had not yet achieved what was necessary for him to take on the mission he was destined for. And so he chose, and Dannion repeated this emphatically, several times, "Death before dishonor." Peter had to go, he said. "It was his time. He is in happiness. Now he is resting."

I didn't know what to make of this. On the plane home, it dawned on me that Dannion had assumed Peter was a teenager. He didn't know that Peter was in his twenty-eighth year. Then, when I got home, I was putting away some of Peter's personal belongings when a letter fell at my feet. It had been written to him by an Army buddy, and written on the envelope were the words "Death Before Dishonor." Coincidences, I said. Yet, somewhat intrigued by this man, two years later, when John and Nancy had been killed and police were making no headway in finding the murderer, I sought out Dannion, visiting him with my sister Jeannette. Remarkably, tuning in to his psychic abilities, he described the killing, the killer, and the time when I would know who did it. I laughed—but only until all he said came true! We later appeared on a segment of television's *Unsolved Mysteries*, when they were doing a story on Dannion's psychic visions.

But back to the trip home from Alabama. I had never been one to take talk of past lives and psychic powers very seriously. Yet after Peter's suicide, I was willing to investigate anything that would shed light on unexplainable human behavior. For about a year, I used the excuse of being a journalist/editor to do, or assign, stories on all kinds of paranormal phenomena, like astrology, dreams, past lives, tarot cards, shamanism, crystals, automatic writing, and psychic powers. While I found nothing disrespectful in all of this, I found something terribly missing—Jesus.

I also felt almost a kind of yearning to study more about Jesus, his life, and his times, to find, if not answers, then consolation, but in a right environment. In effect, I wanted to be in a "safe" place, where I would be assured of truth if I went deeper into a knowledge of Jesus. That summer of 1992, I was reading the *National Catholic Reporter* when I saw an ad that said "Oxford Summer School in Religious Studies." It didn't have much information, but it had a Fordham University telephone number. To this day, I can't explain my action, but I put the paper down, went to the phone, and called.

When I got the further information I had requested, I knew there was another force at work here. Nine exceptional religious educators would be the faculty, one of them being the Very Rev. Dr. N. T. (Tom) Wright, a man considered to be one of the world's outstanding New Testament scholars. If ever there was a person who could bring Jesus alive to others, I felt it would be Dr. Wright. I wasted no time in signing up for what became the most memorable two weeks in my life.

Before I left for England, I had another clue for why I was being drawn to Oxford. This was the place where C. S. Lewis spent most of his life. My son Peter had left me, along with the notes and the tape, three sheets of paper, each with a long quote from C. S. Lewis, about what he believed was our longing for heaven. I think he wanted us to know he died, longing for heaven, by typing out C. S. Lewis's words:

> There have been times when I think we do not desire heaven; but more often I find myself wondering whether, in our heart of hearts, we have ever desired anything else. . . . You would say, "Here at last is the thing I was made for." . . . It is the secret signature of each soul, the incommunicable and unappeasable want, the

thing we desired before we met our wives or made our friends, or chose our work, and which we shall still desire on our deathbeds, when the mind no longer knows wife or friend or work. While we are, this (heaven) is. If we lose this, we lose all.

I had started to read more and more by this devout English author, and now I felt I would learn something more from him at Oxford. I was really taken by this place. Everything at Oxford is old, ancient, stone, mildewed with green moss or covered beautifully with ivy. The dominant feeling for me was that this is a religious place. Steeples, churches, religious imagery is everywhere. The sense of how very major the Christian religion was in past centuries overwhelmed me.

I was overwhelmed, too, as I met the people who were there, like myself, for this summer program in religious studies. One of the first conversations I had was with Dr. John Turner, a six-foot-six Scotsman who was a young Anglican clergyman. I was still in such pain over Peter's death that I couldn't help talking about it. John immediately shared his own experience of pain with me, telling me he had been in a car accident ten years before in which his beloved wife was killed. I told him I was searching to be made whole again. He said this would not happen in any way I thought of at this time. One is so changed by sudden death, he said, that the "alteration" is permanent. You have become a different person by this amputation, one you do not recognize or know. You have first to get to know who this new person is, and then you can start to discover what this new person can be.

In the morning John handed me a note, handwritten on yellow paper, which I cherish. He wrote, "My sister, Time is still new for you since your son's death. Your pain will be with you yet a while. But neither pain nor death is the final thing—the final thing is *life*. I believe with St. Paul that neither life nor death nor any other reality will separate us from the love of God in Jesus Christ. Your son is alive in Jesus Christ as he is in your heart—and in the hearts of your other family members. As an old saint once said, 'All the death that ever was, when put beside all the life there is, would scarcely fill a cup.' All will be well. Blessings on your son. Blessings on your family. Bless you. Your brother in Christ. John"

I knew soon in my trip to Oxford, on my first morning there, that I had come to find Jesus, and I already had.

The organizers of this program, which I found out was offered every summer, had put together an outstanding faculty. I had been particularly drawn to learn about Jesus from the vast knowledge of Dr. Wright, whose newest book, *The New Testament and the People of God*, had just come out. I was in for an impressive surprise. He would be not only a fine teacher but also would become a good friend, inspiring me to continue the search to know Jesus for the rest of my life.

The journalist in me gave me the guts to go right up to him after the first session with him and ask if I could interview him. He warmly agreed. I asked him one question: "What motivated you to write the book?" He said he wanted to find answers for fundamental questions we Christians must ask—How did Christianity begin? What does Christianity believe and does it make sense? In what ways were Christianity and Judaism intertwined in this first generation? And, most important, what sort of authority does the New Testament possess?

Both as a scholar and as a man of faith, he never approached the New Testament as some kind of "magic book," but rather as "a collection of books written at a particular time and by particular people. It should not be treated as though it fell from the sky in the King James Authorized Version, bound in black leather and complete with maps," he said, with his natural good humor. He wanted to get to the "root" of these writings, "back to the start of the whole thing, the original writings of both the early Christians and the Jews of the first century." He was able do these studies in their original languages, being well trained linguistically.

Not too long after beginning these studies Tom Wright realized there was a bigger question to be addressed, "the question of Jesus, every bit a hot potato now as ever. There are several interlocking questions. How did he relate to his Jewish background? What were his actual aims? What was he trying to accomplish? Why did Jesus die? What were the agendas that put him on the cross?

"Then, how do you explain the early Christians? The answer is, you can't, without the resurrection. Something happened on Easter morning. And what that was radically changed the whole world."

He spoke with conviction. "The early church spread like wildfire. Was this an accident? No, the first Christians aimed for this. They were trying to tell people in all corners of society about the god revealed in Jesus. The central Christian claim was that the more we look at Jesus, the more we have to rethink God. They were a group of people grasped by the belief that the hope of Israel had come true, because they saw Jesus to be the new Moses who had produced the new Exodus," redeeming his people from being slaves of the real enemy, Satan. The world, because of Jesus, had become the Promised Land and the early Christians, convinced it was time for the world to see the light, preached this "good news," regarding themselves as a new family, the ones to bring God's word to the world.

I interrupted to ask him about the so-called "hidden years" of Jesus, the mystery of what he was doing from age twelve to about thirty, since nothing is contained in the New Testament about this period of Jesus' life. Dr. Wright said he could shed little light on this. "They remain the silent years. But whatever else Jesus was doing in that period, he got to know the Old Testament like the back of his hand." He used this knowledge "creatively," taking many teachings of the Old Testament, "but giving them a bit of a new twist, authoritatively, to affirm his message.

"I think there is good reason to think Jesus did know he was the Messiah. His message was an invitation to choose a new worldview, a new way of being human."

I knew Dr. Wright had also studied the Dead Sea Scrolls in detail, and so I asked him, do these affirm or deny the New Testament? Saying he had approached the scrolls with excitement and that he loved them, he called them "theological cousins" of the Old Testament, often extremely illuminating as a sidelight to it. But the central claims of Christianity are not, and could not, be undermined by the scrolls.

At the end of my interview in this August of 1992, Tom Wright, a devoted husband and father of four, spoke to me from his heart, telling me that his being drenched in the study of the gospels has had a profound effect on his life. Sometimes in prayer, in some sustained moments where he is focused on the death and resurrection of Jesus, "something about Jesus resonates so powerfully that I must wonder—if this isn't the center of the universe, what is?" That question has lingered in my soul ever since.

Sometimes I get to know that everything we do, all the choices we make, have something of a connection with what's to come. Three years after this first encounter with Dr. Wright, we were in touch again, this time because he was coming to the United States to do a series of lectures in twenty major cities, sponsored by the Oxford Summer School in Religious Studies. He was speaking on the question of "Who Is Jesus?" specifically to take issue with the claims of the Jesus Seminar, a group of academic scholars who get together and vote on whether they think the Bible texts are true or false. I had read some of their writings and found them mostly distressing. My reaction had been a rather angry, "Don't mess with my Jesus."

By this time, Dr. Wright had left his position at Oxford to become Dean of the Cathedral in Lichfield, England. The name struck me because I had been the executive editor of a newspaper in Connecticut called the *Litchfield County Times,* named after the English town, but with an addition, a "t." When Cathy Wilson, director of the Oxford summer program called to tell me about these lectures, I suggested getting a lecture offered in Litchfield, Connecticut, offering to help with publicity both locally and nationally, through Catholic News Service. Dr. Wright then came to speak in my locality for two consecutive years, spreading light on the "Who Is Jesus?" question.

He honestly admitted that scholars have a rough road in going back to that first century, because of the "thinness of the material." People who study ancient history have a fair amount of archaeological evidence, "but little of that comes to the aid of New Testament scholars. Again and again, if we want to ask a fuller set of historical questions, we have to be honest and say we don't know the answers. Some are vaguely possible, some likely and some improbable." Still, he believes, the greater problem would be to avoid history, "for then we would run the risk of creating a Jesus in our own image, so as to sustain our own ideology. I take the gospels extremely seriously. They're talking about something that went on in the real world. The gospels are really biography as well as faith documents," he insisted.

The Jesus Seminar, which dates back to 1985, on the other hand, regards much of the gospels as "theological fiction." They deconstruct much of what Jesus said and did. "The gospel is good news, but they say all Jesus had was good advice," said Dr. Wright, who explained that the approach of the Jesus Seminar has been "to make Jesus a rather folksy, savvy sage who peppers the air with cryptic sayings, and eventually gets himself killed by the authorities."

This is vastly different from the real Jesus of history, who was redefining the Kingdom, radically subverting the Jewish tradition, saying "you as a people are going in the wrong direction." He preached that they must become the people of God in a radically new way, telling them "the Kingdom of God is being established here and now, and anyone who comes my way is welcome!" This was Good News, not sound bites. Then, as Tom Wright so rightly points out, "a crucified Messiah is a failed Messiah," so why wasn't Jesus buried and forgotten? The answer is because Jesus was indeed the Messiah, and proof lies in the resurrection, he says, countering the Jesus Seminar claim that Jesus stayed dead. "The tomb was empty. Jesus' body had been transformed . . . there was no precedent for this and there remains no other instance of this happening to another," Dr. Wright affirmed.

I've had a book for a long time about Jesus that was written by a Cambridge scholar named T.R. Glover nearly one hundred years ago. What he wrote way back then parallels what Tom Wright says.

> Take away the resurrection, however it happened, whatever it was, and the history of the church is unintelligible. . . . We have to find, somewhere or other, between the crucifixion and the first preaching of the disciples in Jerusalem, something that entirely changed the character of that group of men.
>
> *Something happened*, so tremendous and so vital, that it changed not only the character of the movement and the men—but with them the whole history of the world. The evidence for the

79

resurrection is not so much what we read in the gospels as what we find in the rest of the New Testament—the new life of the disciples. They are a new group.

My son Peter had well understood this. I cherish a paper I found among his belongings after his death. He had written it back in 1983, when he was just twenty, for a college history class, eleven years before I went to Oxford. He wrote:

Christ's spirit is sublime. Christ's influence was so great that it split time. He gave the world a message, a blueprint for how people should live and treat each other. People were inspired. From that point, the scope and extent of Christian growth is staggering. Untold numbers of believers died heroically for their faith. So impressive were the many who gladly died for Christ that they were more than replaced by fresh converts. In the fourth century, apostolic Christianity had conquered a great empire.

The sublime Christian spirit is seen in the inspired life works of people like St. Francis, St. Augustine, Gregory the Great, St. Ignatius, John XXIII, and Mother Teresa. The same spirit inspired people to build great cathedrals, pushing the technology of arch and buttress beyond the known limits. From that spirit rose the great religious Orders which still today are leading organizations of humanitarian and social services. Even exploration was greatly inspired by the desire to spread Christ's message.

The skeptical may brush off the miracles of Christianity as good public relations, but there is one basic, undeniable miracle: that the small, motley, demoralized group that Jesus left on earth after his reported ascension developed the enthusiasm to sweep all obstacles before them in their bold worldwide mission. A few disheartened followers were transformed into the most dynamic movement in the history of Mankind.

This is what Peter had come to see as the legacy of Jesus.

My two weeks at Oxford remain memorable forever for me, not only for my encounter with Tom Wright, but also for what I learned from the other members of the faculty. I was especially moved by the very human lectures of the Right Rev. Richard Holloway, Bishop of Edinburgh.

He would surprise us with statements like, "Religion is not about teaching people to be moral. It's about the love of man for God, meeting with love of God for man. Only God can achieve this sublime and irrational relationship." He said that "humor is an important element in faith. It can rescue us from our obsessions and self-absorptions." He acknowledged how difficult life can be, saying "the universe didn't come with an explanatory leaflet attached. Christ is encountered, never explained."

Bishop Holloway didn't hesitate to talk about the times he had found "meanness of spirit in professional religion; for example, the refusal to let a suicide be buried in sacred ground." I later spoke with him about suicide, crying my eyes out for my Peter, then dead only seventeen months, telling him how grateful I was that the Catholic church no longer held to such punishments for suicide. He said that after we acknowledge the loss and wounding when a loved one dies, we must "gather together the life to affirm, and conclude it." And he wanted me to know that if the day came when my pain ended, I might also mourn that, for sometimes subconsciously, people feel that all that's left of their loyalty to the dead is their pain. But that's not true. "We must be the celebrants of their lives," and then they will always be remembered.

His empathy for my very evident pain was not lost on me, especially when he told me a story, quoting C. S. Lewis, who said, "The dead send a gift back to us." He spoke of a man in Scotland who had a wife he so very dearly loved. They lived in the country and she loved to ride her horse, a beautiful white animal. Sadly she died, and mourning her, he would sometimes walk in loneliness on their land. One day, when he was particularly pained, wanting to see her again, he became overwhelmed with the doubt that life went on, fearing the grave was the end. Suddenly, a white horse, riderless, galloped across the fields, disappearing into the distance. He knew that she had sent him a message that she was not on this earth, but she was alive.

I was so very comforted by that story. I had come to Oxford to get to God in an authentic, solid way, but that didn't mean I was going to stop seeking "signs" of our connection to loved ones in heaven. To my surprise I found that being in England was the perfect place to be if I wanted to hear stories of otherworldly phenomenon. In fact, I even went on the "Oxford Ghost Tour," which promised to have us trembling "to the sinister tales of Oxford's Own Vampire, The Headless King and The Haunted Pubs & Colleges." Best thing about this was that I remembered C. S. Lewis used to go to a pub with his buddies and, with no trouble at all since everybody in Oxford knew where it was, I found it. Not only that, I was invited to sit in the very place where this great author sat, sharing some good stuff to drink with his buddies. I looked to heaven and said to Peter, look at me now, kid, and tell C. S. Lewis, thanks.

Another welcome surprise came from Bishop Kallistos Timothy Ware, a lecturer in Eastern Orthodox Studies, who was one of our professors. I was sitting next to him at lunch in mid-week and we started discussing angels. To my happy surprise, he said he believed in them even though "most of my colleagues at Oxford no doubt would not." He then told me a charming story of another Orthodox bishop who was baptizing four children in a family, with ages from about three or four to nine. To make sure they would be quiet, he told them nicely that when they got baptized, they would get a guardian angel, and they wouldn't want to disturb their new guardian angel with noise.

At the end of the ceremony, the youngest child, with his face beaming, asked the Bishop, in all seriousness, "Which of the four angels," and he pointed out a position, "is mine?" Bishop Kallistos said he had no doubt that the child saw angels, even though no one else, the Bishop included, was given that privilege.

I cut class one morning. I had a very strong feeling that I should find a church and pray. Not too far away from where I was staying I reached the Church of St. Mary Magdalene, and went in, feeling I would find something there for me. On the right side of the main church was the Lady's chapel and it had a most unusual three-dimensional Pieta, the length of the altar. I decided this was the place where I should be, for certainly I could relate to Mary, seeing her holding her broken, dead Son. I knew her pain, as she knew mine. We both had screamed from the dark place of seeing a lifeless son. Talking to her, I had an intensely moving meditation and experience, too personal to relate, but I knew then that my coming to this church was no accident.

Nor was it an accident that I happened to pick up a book of literature and found in it some works of Frederick William Faber, a nineteenth-century Oxford scholar who, inspired and guided by John Cardinal Newman, converted to Catholicism. He was noted for his Book of Hymns and other devotional books, most notably *At the Foot of the Cross*. I began to read the section called "The Crucifixion:"

> The Three-and-Thirty Years are ending. A new epoch in the world's history is to open. . . . What will Mary herself be like without Jesus? . . . The Father held Mary up in His arms, lest she should perish under the load of love; and the loud cry went out from the hilltop, hushing Mary's soul into an agony of silence, and the Head drooped towards her, and the eye closed, and the Soul passed her, like a flash, and sank into the earth, and a wind arose, and stirred the mantle of darkness, and the sun cleared itself of the moon's shadow, and the roofs of the city glimmered white, and the birds began to sing, but only as if they were half reassured, and Mary stood beneath the Cross a childless Mother.

I had been trying to console myself that I still had six children. I would say that, hoping it would give me strength to rise above my agony of losing Peter. But now I understood. I was, like Mary, a childless mother. I would always be childless on this earth, and Mary would be the one who could really understand. If I ever lost another of my children, I would be childless again, for there is no wholeness for a mother when one child is gone. Yes, the sun comes out again, the roofs of the city can glimmer white and the birds can start singing, but I, like Mary, would know till our last breath that we were both a childless mother, held up only by the love that didn't die with the passing of our child. I had come to Oxford seeking Jesus, and he gave me a bonus. He helped me find, and be comforted by, his Mother, the one person who knew exactly the earthly pain I would forever suffer, who, in empathy, would always be there to hug this childless mother.

The church had been empty, and as I walked down the aisle to leave, I saw a young man, maybe eighteen or so, at the back of the church. He was wearing U.S. Army camouflage clothes, exactly the kind Peter always wore, was built like Peter, and had dark hair like his. I thought this was very strange. As I got closer, he slid to the floor. I smiled at him and then he said, "Mum, do you know Oxford?" I said, "Not well." Then he said something that startled me. He said, "Mum, I just want to go home," adding that he was hungry and had no money. His home was outside of Oxford, he said. I gave him five pounds, put my hand on his head, which was wet— it had been apparently raining—said I hoped this helped and asked him to pray for me.

I think he was one of the million or so homeless at that time in the London area. But it was his first few words that got to me, "Mum, I just want to go home." They reminded me of Peter's words in his last note, saying that "It's time to go home," wanting at last to be, as C. S. Lewis had expressed it, in his "permanent home."

I left Oxford, knowing anew how Jesus is full of surprises in how he gets his ever-present messages of love to us. I could relate ever more firmly to C. S. Lewis when he said: "I believe in Christianity as I believe in the sun—not only because I see it, but because by it I see everything else."

6

Christ's Spirit *Can't Be Killed*

---

*Christ who, being the holiest among
the mighty, and the mightiest among
the holy, lifted with his pierced hands
empires off their hinges and turned the
stream of centuries out of its channel,
and still governs the ages.*

—JOHN PAUL RICHTER

I was a teenager when I first heard of Graham
Greene, the British author, after reading a
newspaper story about his book, *The Power and the
Glory*. I was fascinated because he was a convert to
Catholicism and the book was about the Mexican
government's persecution of priests. Immediately I
started to research and discovered the dark history of
how the Catholic Church had been so viciously
persecuted by official Mexico, especially after

diplomatic relations between Mexico and the Vatican were broken off in 1857.

That year, the man in power, Benito Juarez, incorporated an anti-church constitution to break the power of Roman Catholicism, separating church and state and suppressing religious orders. The persecution of priests was so severe and long-standing that until the 1930s, priests could only function underground. One of the priests, executed in 1927 for his fidelity to Jesus, was Jesuit Father Miguel Pro, along with his brother Humberto, and a close friend, Luis Segura Vilchis. Once I had checked out the history, I didn't bother to read Greene's popular book.

Then some sixteen years later, as Mexico was celebrating the centennial of the anti-church constitution by proclaiming this "The Year of the 1857 Constitution and Liberal Thought," I happened to meet a Latin American priest who was a distant relative of Luis Vilchis. His cousin, he said, was an engineer and a leading member of the Catholic Association of Mexican Youth at the time. Father Pro was considered to be impudent and clever. He did his priestly work night and day in disguise, saying Mass, baptizing babies, hearing confessions and gathering young men to make them active Catholics, keepers and spreaders of the faith. The authorities considered him to be in violation of the constitution. He got in real trouble when Plutarco Elias Calles became president in 1926 and instituted a new wave of Catholic persecution.

On November 13, 1927, a bomb was thrown into a car carrying a general. That became a great excuse for Calles to eliminate Father Pro, his brother, and Luis Vilchis. He accused them of attempted murder. They never had a trial. Six days later, they were brought out of their cells, blinking from the daylight they saw for the first time since their arrest, led to a barricade of logs with three bullet-chipped targets, grotesquely shaped like human forms, pitted with bullet holes from practice sessions. Before each of them was executed by the firing squad, they called out "Viva Christo Rey!" Long Live Christ the King.

The only crime these three young men were guilty of was their love of God and their Catholic faith. They were perfect victims for Calles because their work was well known and their deaths, he surmised, would inspire great terror in the hearts of other Catholics. But, as always, the mystery remains—the more the church is persecuted, the stronger it comes back. As a footnote, Father Pro was beatified on September 25, 1988.

This is the story Graham Greene fictionalized in 1940, judged ever since to be his greatest novel. It was picked up by Hollywood, and Henry Fonda starred in the movie. I got to see it back in the 1960s and while I would be hard-pressed to recall a lot of it, it is the ending that is imprinted in my brain. The priest has been executed, the people are in their church, when a stranger comes to the door. He gives his name. He is the new priest. It is an emotional moment, and one in which the people seem to know—*Christ can't be killed.* That's what Graham Greene was sure of. For me, the scene was utterly powerful. I felt as if I could really understand now the emotions in the upper room when Jesus, his wounds showing, came to let his closest friends know that he could never be killed.

I love a line from a poem by Alfred Tennyson heralding the coming of Christ to this earth—"And so the Word had breath." That sentence links us to the Genesis story of creation, where God breathes into the dust of the earth and creates humanity. How fitting it is that God sends us the Word in the person of his Son, as John's gospel affirms, to show us how to live and breathe. No earthly force can ever kill Christ's spirit, God's breath.

Around the same time that I saw *The Power and the Glory* I happened to come across two books containing an account of the private revelations of Anne Catherine Emmerich, a nineteenth-century German nun and mystic, that made me label Jesus' birth as a decidedly earth-shaking event. According to her writings, she saw the events of the Old and New Testaments as if she were an onlooker, watching as they happened. Her visions, of places she never visited and happenings that took place in a previous time, were quite extraordinary and often verified by scripture, history, and geography, even though they were never taken very seriously by theologians.

After detailed revelations of the childhoods, betrothal, and wedding of Mary and Joseph—she even described Mary's wedding gown—Sister Emmerich "sees" the couple, six months later, enter Bethlehem. She describes how upset and pained Joseph was to think that in his own home town he couldn't even find a room for his young wife who had made a most difficult, long trip at a time when, in her delicate condition, she shouldn't have been traveling at all.

Finally, Joseph tells Mary, apologetically, in Sister Emmerich's vision, that he knows of a place outside of town where they could find shelter, an old shepherd's cave, a hideout where he had often played and prayed as a small boy. If not theological, this was logical, for Joseph was returning to the place of his birth to be registered for the census ordered by the king. Every young boy has his secret hiding places and why should Joseph be an exception? The thought of Jesus being born in a cave where his foster father played as a child struck me as being a rather lovely tribute to Joseph.

Sister Emmerich went into great detail describing Joseph's cave, which she saw as having two "chambers" with walls of natural rock and some rough masonry. She saw a roof of light reeds, supported by posts, extending out from the front entrance for shade.

The "crib" was a "hollowed out stone trough lying on the ground and used for cattle to drink from; over it stood a longish rectangular manger, or rack, narrower below and broader above, made of wooden lattice work and raised on four feet so that the animals could comfortably eat the hay or grass in the rack and lower their heads to drink water in the trough beneath."

She gave this account of the birth of Jesus, as she saw it:

I saw the radiance around the Blessed Virgin ever growing greater. . . . At midnight, she was rapt in an ecstasy of prayer. I saw her lifted from the earth so that I saw the ground beneath her. The radiance around her increased.

Everything, even things without life, were in a joyful, inner motion; the stones of the roof, of the walls and of the floor of the cave became as if they were alive in the light.

Then I no longer saw the roof of the cave; a pathway of light opened above Mary . . . the Blessed Virgin, borne up in ecstasy, was now gazing downwards, adoring her God, whose mother she had become and who lay on the earth before her in the form of a helpless, newborn child.

Anne Catherine Emmerich was a mystic, not a theologian, yet her vision of the birth of Jesus has an unusual profundity about it for believing Christians. For she reveals that God becoming human was an event so powerful that it caused the unseen, minute, all-pervading molecules and atoms of creation to tremble with excitement in the presence of this happening.

That may be more poetry than theology, but her vision of Jesus' birth as an earth-shaking event has ever intrigued me. Jesus' spirit can never be killed. It gives life to the very molecules of earth. It is the *breath*—of all creation, and that includes us. No wonder Jesus could speak in so many ways about how we are all *one* with him and the Father, a truth that underscores how precious we are to him.

No wonder, too, that before Jesus went out to the garden to pray as he waited to be captured and put to death, he gave one last plea to his friends, "Love one another as I have loved you." If I knew I was going to die and had one last chance to say something to the people I cared about and who I hoped would follow me, I would want it to be the most important words from my heart that I could leave with them. I think this was certainly true for Jesus, and so he gave that handful of chosen friends the one-sentence blueprint that explained so simply why they were special and would from now on be their job description. I jotted a line once from a book that said, "Until a man knows Jesus Christ, he has little chance of even guessing the grandeur of which he himself is capable." I think that, in time, those who knew Jesus so closely radiated incredible grandeur, faithful to his legacy right to their deaths, becoming agents who changed the course of history.

I have met people who radiate the grandeur of Jesus, none more sparkling than Sister Mary Antoinette of the Daughters of Wisdom. I had met her when I was a reporter with *The Long Island Catholic* in 1963. She was on a brief summer visit home after working two years in the Congo, at Isangi, an inland post 120 miles from Stanleyville, up the river by flatboat. That summer there were eleven Daughters of Wisdom in Isangi from Holland, Belgium, France, Italy, America, and three Congolese nuns conducting an 800-pupil school, an orphanage, and a hospital.

Conditions were so desperate at the mission that Sister Mary Antoinette spent her few weeks here trying to raise material aid. I got to meet her, and we became instant friends, beginning with the fact that we shared the same name. She told me, "I'll make no bones about it. Our need is money. The slums in New York would be for the African a sign of wealth. Our children are starving. We're grateful for a few bags of rice or potatoes even if they are so wormy that the stuff walks in by itself."

I wrote a feature story on her, and she told of her need. The article brought in some money, supplies, and contacts with some key people at Catholic Relief Services and International Catholic Charities in New York. I was happy about that but not at all at ease in what she told me in our time together about the dangers she faced back in the Congo, which was in an "economic, social, and moral degeneration after two years of a chaotic independence."

Sister Mary Antoinette knew the score, knew she was going back to trouble, and she was nervous about it. I remember how she kept twisting her handkerchief. But nothing would change her mind about going back. She was returning to a hostile place where she was not wanted, not thanked, not respected, in spite of all her good work over so many years. Even one-time youngsters who had been taught and nursed by the nuns were coming back to taunt them, telling them to go away and not come back. Their new independence was "a complicated toy which they hadn't yet learned how to handle," as she put it.

"So why do we stay?" she went on. "People have said, 'Aren't you stupid. You don't get paid and you don't get enough to eat. You could teach in a beautiful high school here.' True. But if everybody pulled out of Africa, what would happen to the church there? How could God's work be fulfilled?"

I marveled at her, that in the face of so much personal danger, she was so unshakably committed to her work, doing what she believed was Jesus' work, carried out through his Mystical Body. She went back to Isangi, telling me, "I've got to go back. My children need me. I don't know what's facing me back in the Congo. We have no recourse but patience."

Seventeen months later, on November 19, 1964, we found out what she faced. She was murdered, as was Sister Marie Francoise, by Congolese rebels. Hostages who had been rescued reported she had been "subjected to degrading humiliation, beaten with rifle butts, sticks and machetes, her body thrown into the Congo River." She wanted always to do Jesus' work and she carried on, like him—to the death.

One of the last things she said to me before she went back to Isangi was that she never felt their work was wasted. "I don't know the ending, but what we do is a beginning," she said. Her words were strongly reminiscent of words spoken by another strong person who was murdered, President John F. Kennedy: "Our work will not be finished in the first hundred days. Nor will it be finished in the first thousand days, not even in our lifetime on this planet, but let us begin."

Time and again throughout history, stories have surfaced which show that in spite of attempts by ruling powers to destroy the presence of Christ, the carpenter survives. Just as he confounded Pilate, Herod, and the Romans who thought they silenced him forever by killing him, he comes back ever alive to seed the hearts of people over and over with his spirit that brings a message of faith, justice, mercy, and everlasting life.

History records such times so frequently. Years ago I read of a law in colonial times that tried to suppress the spirit of Christ in the person of priests trying to bring the sacraments to the few Catholics then in the New World. New York State in the 1700s had ruled it a crime, punishable by death, to be a "papist priest." One priest used to travel incognito, disguised as "Dr. Schneider" to bring the sacraments to clusters of Catholics as far away as Pennsylvania.

Because of the uncertainty of the times, with his life in danger from the natural elements to the ruling governors, "Dr. Schneider" taught one group of German Catholics in Pennsylvania to say the rosary every day as a way of holding on to the faith. Many years later, these Catholics, who by that time had not seen a priest in over two generations, still said the rosary and their faith in Jesus and the church was strong.

Well known is the story of the "secret Christians" of Japan, a community of some 30,000 people on the Goto Islands who are the direct descendents of the first Japanese to be converted to Christianity by St. Francis Xavier in the sixteenth century. They persevered in keeping the faith through three centuries of persecution.

In 1982 I had the privilege of meeting and interviewing Paul M. Tagita of Japan visiting at the Abbey of Regina Laudis in Bethlehem, Connecticut. He had managed to become a friend of the "secret Christians" of Japan in 1926 and was the first to write about these people. He told me it was the deaths of his parents during his twenties that put him on a quest to study religion and that's when he uncovered the "secret Christians." Even though they were badly treated, being forced to bow before the Shinto shrine under pain of death, they held to their belief in Christ for three centuries. Though Mr. Tagita was a Congregationalist, he became very sympathetic to the Catholics, and was very happy when a thesis he wrote about them won him a scholarship to do a three year study of the "secret Christians."

His research affected him in a profound way, making him ever a religious seeker, leading him to become a Buddhist. But that was only a step on the real journey, this gentle man, then eighty-five, told me, with a smile. He had several encounters with Franciscan priests, one of them Father Maximillian Kolbe, which, in 1938, led to his conversion to Catholicism, along with his wife and four children. Father Kolbe was the priest in Hitler's death camps who took the place of a father who was to be killed, giving up his life for another, the ultimate act of love, according to Jesus. He has been beatified by the church.

Mr. Tagita had yet to face more suffering. He was teaching near Nagasaki when the atom bomb fell on August 9, 1945. Tears fell from his eyes as he spoke about the horror of this destruction and loss of lives. It made him a seeker for peace ever since. "The necessity we have now is to love—to love or die." Those were his words.

I spoke for two hours with Mr. Tagita, and knew I was in the presence of a very holy man.

We are never at a loss for stories of how Christ's spirit can't be killed. I remember an item in the *Wall Street Journal* that caught my eye some twenty years ago. It was headlined "Dangerous Characters" and told about the sentencing of three men in Czechoslovakia convicted of a "misdeed against the interests of socialist society." This was before the fall of Communism. They were sent to jail for thirty-two months, four years, and five years. Their crime? Smuggling rosaries, crucifixes, and chalices into Czechoslovakia from Poland.

On first reading, I shook my head, and from the vantage point of being in a free country, I felt like laughing—or maybe crying—to think possession of such otherworldly items could possibly be considered a crime. What was it about rosaries, crucifixes, and chalices that so badly frightened then socialist Czechoslovakia? What could possibly have been dangerous about them?

The answer was sad and obvious. The government had to keep out anything that could infect the head and the soul with beliefs, ideals, and dreams contrary to the socialist system they had set up. Obviously, they were not trying to keep the country untouched by rosaries from Poland, but by something much more serious. They had to keep out the *spirit* of Poland, namely Jesus, so reflected in the rosaries, crucifixes, and chalices.

The fidelity of the people of Poland to Christianity is recorded in history, standing in glaring contradiction to those who would have destroyed their Christ spirit, if they could have, through the centuries. This was eloquently expressed in book called *A Freedom Within*, the prison notes of Stefan Cardinal Wyscynski, an outspoken critic of the Communist regimes, who died in 1981. His own words explain why the repressive Czechoslovakian government would be afraid of rosaries, crucifixes, and chalices:

> The cause of Christ has existed almost two thousand years, and people are still in prisons for it today. The cause has survived. It is alive, fresh, young, full of allure. How many guards have changed, prisons have fallen into ruin, keys have rusted, chains and locks have been removed—yet the cause endures.

This is true because of what is at the very heart of the Christian experience—that because of Jesus, God and humankind came in touch with each other, bringing about a new union between God and his people. From now on, the guesswork about creation would be gone. Jesus had shown us how we are supposed to live, from God's outlook. The amazing truth he presented was that it is all so simple. Over and over Jesus explained that the design, the pattern, the work, the relationships, everything about how we should live our lives is contained in one word—love. But then came the clincher. It had to be loving one another *as he had loved us.*

For two thousand years, we've been inundated with falling grades, leaving centuries full of debris left by hate. Yet, Jesus lives. He's in the person who was here yesterday, is here today, and will be here tomorrow. I see him in a young priest telling me of a sad experience he had had the day before. A young, Hispanic man had come to the church to see a priest. He wasn't a parishioner and was unknown to the priest. He was in great distress, crying. His mother had died that day.

The priest tried to give him some empathetic comfort, but it didn't really help. The youth was crying because his mother had died, and he had no money to buy her some flowers.

Why were the flowers so important? The priest didn't bother to ask. Instead, he went to the altar, took the two beautiful vases of flowers that had been placed there for Sunday morning Mass and gave them to the young man. He told me, "You have no idea how happy he was as he walked out with those two huge pots of flowers. Can you imagine what it must be like to be so poor that your mother dies and you can't buy her a flower?"

It was Jesus asking that question, and then answering it with love.

7

The Jesus Who Sought to

End the Horror of War

Someday people will want peace so badly that governments had better get out of their way and let them have it.

—DWIGHT D. EISENHOWER

As a kid growing up, every year at the end of May my father would see to it that I went to the parade for the holiday that was then called "Decoration Day." Once, when I was very young, I asked him why that name. He said it was because this was the day people were supposed to remember the soldiers who had died in all the American wars ever fought, go to cemeteries and "decorate" their graves. We needed a holiday, he said, to make sure the sacrifices of the soldiers were never forgotten.

I didn't know then that war was soon to become the dominating reality of my life—starting with an atrocity at Pearl Harbor as I became an adolescent. At first the rallying cry of U.S. patriotism had a romanticism about it. Still young, we chanted hate-German, hate-Japanese slogans, cheered the young men in their glamorous uniforms, crunched cans for recycling, counted ration stamps, and bought war bonds.

It was later that the charm turned sour, when we saw our high schools become nearly all-girl classes because the boys wanted to "sign up" for the war—and we watched the first flag-draped coffin come into the church. I can't remember the names of many of my high school classmates, but I remember, by name, the first of the boys in the Cathedral Academy who went from basketball to Okinawa and elsewhere and never again walked the halls with classmates. Their pictures, for us never to forget, were in our yearbook—Bill Rossi, Sal Andrews, Bill Riley, Tony Lenge, Frank Horwedel, John Grinrod, Roy Marshall.

We, the teenagers of the 1940s, were old before our time. I would look at the grieving mothers and could see so clearly that they had expected to raise their sons for *life,* never dreaming they would meet death in their teens and twenties, before they had a chance to really live, drawn by force into chaos and destruction brought on by war. For me, so young then, war itself became the enemy.

By 1944, we had all gotten so weary of war and the deaths of U. S. soldiers. We wanted a bomb that would put an end to it—and we got it with the unleashing of the atomic bomb on Hiroshima and Nagasaki. With few exceptions the American people applauded President Harry S. Truman's order. History books record that when he got the news of the bombing, President Truman "exultantly exclaimed, 'This is the greatest thing in history.'" Few would have contradicted him back then.

What had been initiated, of course, was the arms race competition with the most destructive weapons known to man. Whereas before, we could blow up cities, now our atomic bombs and their successors, nuclear weapons, would be able to disintegrate the entire global universe—as repeated headlines have reminded us regularly since then.

World War II, even while it was being fought, was touted to be "the war to end all wars," yet just five years after it ended, the Korean War had descended upon us. I had that year given birth to a son. Now the reality of war was different for me. I felt that if the "war to end all wars" had failed to do just that, as Korea indicated, war would be always in our future. I would look at my baby son and see so clearly that I wanted to raise him for life, not death, to see him add to the beauty and peace of this world and not be drawn into its chaos and destruction.

And so, for me, war itself then became the enemy, as I truly believed was just what Jesus had proclaimed, not in so many specific words, but in his very mission. He had come to change the old world order, which throughout history from the dawn of creation had been one of violence and war, to make it one of peace originating in the hearts and heads of people. But who was paying attention?

War, the enemy, was solidified for me when they brought Harley home in a body bag. He was a farm boy, one of my students in the high school in Cape Vincent, New York where I taught the year before my first son was born. I can never forget Harley, with his droll sense of humor and his budding life, only three years younger than I was back in 1951, when his life ended on a freezing battlefield in Korea.

By the time Vietnam exploded, I was the mother of seven, five of them sons, and an activist in the peace movements. My adopted son Sterling was older and married, but my two sons Paul and John were now eligible for the perverted glory of serving in Vietnam. I found myself sitting with my reporter pad and pencil often in the homes of mourning families of a POW or MIA or a dead son. I concluded that the Vietnam War was also a mothers' war.

The toughest interview I ever did was with a mother whose son was killed in Chulai on August 20, 1967. That death blasted her life and made her a mourner, along with her raging thoughts—"Now we've killed Jimmy Woods, my son. Time should have stood still. The earth should have quaked. Or, at least, a war should have stopped," she told me. But nothing more happened than a burial. The world wasn't better for his death. And Billie Woods, Gold Star Mother, refused to settle for what had happened. She told me Jimmy was the friendly, blue-eyed kid who worked at a hamburger stand and had a girlfriend and plans for marriage. "He had to go half way around the world to find an enemy," she said.

Billie Woods used every cent of the Army insurance money to fight her own private battle with the government. She petitioned officials to make the date of her son's death a national holiday. He was a hero, she said. He should be honored. The country should take a day off to remember him as a person, with a name, her son, now dead.

I interviewed her in a shopping center where she campaigned for help in her fight to get June 5—Jimmy's birthday—set aside each year and declared as a "United Peace and Honor Jimmy Woods Day."

Billie Woods didn't win her private battle. She was called crazy and only touched a few people, like me. A couple of years later, when I waited, with agitation in my chest, for the numbers to be called—the draft lottery that held the destiny of individual young men, among them two of my sons—I thought of Billie Woods and I knew she had been right all along. She wasn't crazy.

Like me, she had given birth to her children for them to live, not die. I was lucky. For both my sons, the numbers were high. They were not summoned to Vietnam. The draft lottery saved them from the death lottery.

But Billie Woods had opened my eyes to the pain of a mother who survives the death of a child of any age. I learned from her that if our child dies, we have to find some meaning in their death to keep from going crazy. Billie Woods was not crazy; she was trying to keep from going crazy! I was there, in that place, twenty-five years later, when the First Gulf War was launched. But my story is different.

In late summer of 1989, I was working at my editor's job at my office in Connecticut when a call came in from Elizabeth Knappman, a literary agent and author I had become friendly with after reviewing two of her books. She told me that a publisher, Facts on File, was putting out a series of books on America at War and wanted to know if I would be interested in writing the one on World War I. Normally, I would have said, "No way. I don't know enough about that war and don't have time to research it." But for some unknown reason, I said, "Let me think about it."

Within a few days I received a call from my son Peter from Guam, where he had been teaching math. He was in enormous pain, again battling the destructive chemicals in his brain. He said he had resigned from his Catholic school teaching position as head of the math department and would be coming home. As most mothers would know, his pain was always my pain, and I was begging heaven again to show me a way to help my son. When Peter arrived home, it was clear to me he was discouraged, and also worried about finding work. Suddenly, remembering how he was an expert on war— I think he had studied every war that had taken place from the dawn of humankind—I got a brainstorm. "Peter," I asked, "how would you like to write a book on

World War I?" His face brightened. "I'd love it," he answered.

I called Elizabeth the next day, and assured her that Peter really could do the book, that he had tremendous knowledge about that war and great writing skills. She trusted me, put Peter in touch with John Bowman, the editor, and he immediately went to work. I was soon to see just how much Peter did know about that war. I offered to type his chapters since he was a poor typist, and as he would read me what he wrote, he would embellish the stories, telling me details that he couldn't put into the book because of length limitations. I knew he suffered intense pain for the insanity, the madness, the deaths, the horrors of those four years from 1914 to 1918.

Peter, like myself and my other children, had always abhorred war, but now I was beginning to really understand how personally my son took the killings. I also knew—because he talked so much about it—how he had been obsessed with the Holocaust and the inhuman deaths of millions by the hands and machines of humans in World War II. He had shocked me when, on his eighteenth birthday, April 25, 1981, he had gone to the Army Recruiting office and joined the U.S. Army. He told me later he was supposed to be sent to South Korea, but he had managed to get the orders changed. "I had to go to Germany," he told me. As for why Germany was so important, I got a clue when my son, home on a visit, told me he had gone to shrines and cemeteries in Germany on his knees, praying in reparation for the deaths of both the Jewish and the German people that were caused by the satanic Holocaust.

Peter finished the book on World War I and quickly wrote two others, one on the War of 1812 and the other on the lost colony of Virginia, another "holocaust" from another time. He was awaiting publication of all three when the Gulf War started in January 1991, and that's when I began to see a major depression set in. He was especially distressed when he came to me, waving a newspaper, quoting the lines of the elder President George Bush that this is "a just war, about good and evil, right versus wrong." He noted that Saddam Hussein had long been saying this is "a Holy War . . . the people of God against the infidels and the Satan in Washington." What a mockery of truth when two heads of state start battling, both claiming that God is on their side, he remarked.

Because he studied history so seriously—and had a brain that retained everything he studied—Peter talked about the complex, fuzzy relations that had preceded this war—who we supported and why, who we ignored and why. He felt the administration had dishonestly turned this into a cops and robbers, cowboys and Indians, the good guys against the bad guys theater. It was very clear, of course, in the United States who was wearing the white hats. He was so disturbed to see a boy, maybe eight or nine on TV, being asked about the war. Proudly, the boy said, "We're there to kick some butt." He's "following the wrong leaders," Peter said, profoundly sad, saying the voice of sanity was that of Pope John Paul II. Before the Gulf War was launched the Pontiff had made a plea to the President: "Save humanity the tragic experience of a new war. A war would not resolve the problems, only aggravate them."

My son started to became quiet, often appeared to be in a hurry, on the excuse that he was trying to meet a deadline for his "lost colony" book. He would be distressed that we were killing people "and this time for oil," he would say. He wondered what Jesus was thinking, looking down and seeing that "man's inhumanity to man was once again taking over." As the dead servicemen and women began coming back home in body bags, this tragedy worked on his brilliant, moral, fragile brain. Then, like the force of a volcanic eruption, he left this earth, on March 18, 1991.

We listened to his voice on the tape he left, and it broke my heart to know that war had contributed to his terminal pain:

> I am a student of history and of the many lessons to be learned from the past, two hit the hardest for me, and that is, one, that there has been immeasurable suffering. And two, that most suffering has been brought about by humans upon their fellow humans. Perhaps this is a lopsided view from too much concentration on warfare, but wars do happen and with greater frequency than the average person realizes.
>
> All the many wars were propagated and executed by people who thought drastically different from me and therein lies the problem. I believe that inhumanity is wrong and I'm not alone. But history shows that I'm in the minority. Let us consider the war against Iraq. In this neo-imperialist conflict, my country beat up a former client state mercilessly and without pity. Well, it's not the first time I've been mortified by the actions of my government, but this was different. I've always thought, oh, government is corrupt and greedy and all that, but this was different. In this crisis I gained a lot of insight on the American public, and I don't like what I saw. I can respect differences in opinion, but the mood of most of my countrymen, the norm, is a fundamental antithesis to my own values . . . and this has been a blow to me.

As a family, we shed tons of tears. We never judged Peter. While we all hated war, we were grateful none of us had battling brain chemicals that would drive us to kill ourselves because of war. I knew Peter wasn't the first to do so. During the Vietnam War I had worked in human rights, specifically trying to help the poor and the migrant workers in Suffolk County, Long Island, with a Lutheran minister, a father, so concerned for others, so deeply sensitive to inhumanity. One day the war overtook him. He connected a hose to the tailpipe of his car, started the engine, and breathed in the fumes until he had no more breath. Like Peter, he, too, could become a casualty of a world that had not honored the nonviolence and peace that Jesus lived and died for.

I have been challenged by some who do not really believe that the peace Jesus spoke of has anything to do with not going to war. How can you prove this, they ask? And I answer, "Listen to Jesus and observe his actions. For starters, let's go back to World War I, where his name is Benedict XV and John XXIII."

Because of Peter, I have really come to know World War I well. Shortly before the massacre at the World Trade Center on September 11, 2001, I received a call out of the blue from John Bowman, Peter's editor, telling me that the publisher was putting their America at War books out in expanded editions. Peter was the only deceased author, and since they knew me to be a writer, they gave me the option of taking on this task. I said yes, gratefully, to keep Peter's name on that book.

I truly met Jesus in the research that followed, never more alive than in the man named Cardinal Giacomo Della Chiesa, who was elected pope in September 1914, a month following the beginning of the "Great War," taking the name Benedict XV. He tried to make the world see how the warring countries had created a "horrendous bloodbath which dishonors Europe," and had turned the world into "a hospital and a cemetery." He tried to make the countries see how they were carrying out the "darkest tragedy of human hatred and human madness" with this "useless massacre."

While the countries continued the killing, Pope Benedict poured out love. He established an "Office for Prisoners" in the Vatican, making it possible for prisoners of war, and soldiers at the front, on all sides, as far as possible, to maintain contact with their families; he gave money to set up welfare works for war victims, in all countries, getting them food, warm clothing, and medical care; he insisted on help worldwide to ease the pain and deprivations being endured by the innumerable widows and orphaned children suffering hunger and homelessness. Later, he found a way to have the Vatican raise five million lire to help those starving from the Russian famine. In his efforts to relieve the suffering on all sides during this war, he spent some 82 million lire, an enormous amount of money back then, and was criticized for nearly bankrupting the Vatican. But Pope Benedict, emphasizing Christian love, proclaimed that "It is the duty of every person to run to help another human being who is in danger of death,"— *and I, personally, have never heard a better definition of peace!*

That war was to have a great effect on another man of God, a young priest by the name of Angelo Roncalli who was assigned to a medical unit in a military hospital in Milan. His biographer Alden Hatch wrote:

> The war was a time of intense suffering for Don Angelo, a time of testing and of learning through sorrow. The military hospitals in which he worked were extremely primitive at best. There were no sulfa drugs to cleanse the wounds, and the long wards were foul with the smell of putrid flesh and loud with the shrieks and groans of men crazed by fever or, less mercifully, fully conscious of their condition...
>
> He also served on the terrible battlefields. Pope John [spoke] of that time as the most moving experience of his long life. In the rain and mud of the dreadful spring of 1917, his cassock stained with blood, he moved among the troops on the plateau of Asiago and the blood-soaked fields along the Piave bringing help and comfort to the

wounded, and, [in his words] "to the dying, the last consolations of friendship and the reconciliation of final absolution."

Roncalli said long afterward, "I thank God that I was a sergeant and a military chaplain in World War I. How much I learned of the human heart at that time; how much experience I gained; how much grace I received."

Like Pope Benedict, the young priest called this war "a useless massacre." Influenced by the Pope, he founded a "House for the Soldiers," and worked to search for soldiers unaccounted for. Clearly, as he brought the love of Jesus to the soldiers, the seeds were sown here for his yearning that there would one day be *pacem in terris*—peace on earth.

Just as Jesus was ignored, denied, even ridiculed, so was Pope Benedict, who was literally written off as he tried so hard to get the nations killing millions in World War I to stop. He was not even given the courtesy of being a part of the talks that produced the infamous Treaty of Versailles, which in the end, gave all the spoils to the "winners." The French and British governments went for revenge and punishment, humiliating Germany by making it take full moral and financial responsibility for the war. They carved up the Middle East to solidify their colonial empires. Seeing "revenge, greed and stupidity" in the abominable treaty, the Pope said, sounding like Jesus, "Nations do not die; in humiliation and revenge, they pass from generation to generation the sorrowful heritage of hatred and retaliation."

Pope Benedict had argued that if a peace settlement was not built on Christian principles of justice, and above all, charity, latent hostilities between peoples would rise again and there could be no real reconciliation and therefore no lasting peace. His words were prophetic. A German Army corporal who had been wounded, and gassed in battle, almost losing his eyesight, was determined to settle scores and regain all and more that Germany had lost at Versailles. His name was Adolf Hitler. World War I's most devastating legacy was to become the cause of World War II. Pope Benedict, the man who followed Jesus and predicted the woe to come from not seeking true peace, didn't live to see the horror that had been sown with that Versailles Treaty of June 28, 1919. He died on January 22, 1922.

Don Angelo Roncalli, however, was still to live through that war, whose seeds had been sown at Versailles. He was carrying out an assignment as Apostolic Delegate to Turkey as World War II broke out. In constant contact with the Vatican, he assisted many Jewish refugees in escaping from the Nazis and finding asylum in Palestine, notably signing false certificates of baptism for Jewish children. At this time no one could have imagined that this man would one day become Pope John XXIII and cause what some people have called "an earthquake" in the church. He had met his "brothers and sisters" in human misfortune, and he wanted to bring Christ's healing to all by seeking peace and justice throughout the whole world. When he opened the Second Vatican Council, he addressed a special audience, telling them he was burning with "the desire to work and to suffer so that the hour would come when Jesus' prayer at the Last Supper—'that all may be one'—would become a reality for all."

His permanent gift to the world is a document he called *Pacem in Terris*, which is a gospel for all times, a declaration of the "good news" that can come to a world if it chooses a new social order, one "founded on truth, built according to justice, vivified and integrated by charity and put into practice in freedom." He said, "Justice, right reason, and humanity demand that the arms race should cease . . . that nuclear weapons should be banned . . . and that a general agreement should be reached about progressive disarmament and an effective method of control."

He said that citizens should share in their own government and that nations should cooperate in common endeavors to eliminate evils, such as the stockpiling of war materials, harsh treatment of political prisoners, and the industrial dislocation of workers. Always, he emphasized, international disputes should be settled by negotiation rather than by war. He underscored that reflection on the horrors of nuclear war should lead all people more earnestly to seek peaceful solutions to political problems. He explicitly congratulated the United Nations for its work, and especially for its "Universal Declaration of Human Rights," which he called a powerful document in its recognition of the dignity of human persons.

Two years later, his appeal for peace was underscored in another document, the *Pastoral Constitution on the Church in the Modern World:* "The arms race is one of the greatest curses on the human race and the harm it inflicts on the poor is more than can be endured . . . let us . . . find ways of resolving controversies in a manner worthy of human beings. Providence urgently demands of us that we free ourselves from the age-old bondage of war."

Just as Jesus had his detractors, so did Pope John. Some thought his encyclical would give a boost to the Communist Party, saying "pacem in terris" was really "falcem in terris." Some praised it as embodying the best hopes of humankind and called it "revolutionary." Pope John himself, seeking the brotherhood of all, in all places of the world, hoped it would be thought of as "evolutionary."

The Popes who succeeded him, Paul VI and John Paul II, both followed with urgent and uncompromising messages of peace, saying "War never again!" Pope John Paul's writings on peace are legion, none more chilling than his words in *Centesimus Annus,* as the first Gulf War came to a close: "War destroys the lives of the innocent; it teaches killing and throws even the lives of killers into confusion. It leaves behind a trail of rancor and hate, making it harder to achieve a just solution of the problems that provoked it."

As talk of a second Gulf War intensified, John Paul II again spoke out forcefully: "Nothing is resolved through reprisal and retaliation. No one can remain silent and inactive—no political or religious leader. *It seems that war has been declared on peace!*" In spite of his efforts to avert another war, even sending his delegate, Cardinal Pio Laghi, to urge President George Bush to work with the United Nations to find a peaceful solution to America's issues with the Iraqi leader Saddam Hussein, the Pope was soundly ignored by Bush. On March 9, 2003, ten days before America, Great Britain, and its "coalition" invaded Iraq, the Pope gave a Lenten address, using strong words: "The choice between peace and war is also a choice between good and evil that calls all Christians, especially in this Lenten period, to reject the temptations of Satan, as Jesus did in the desert." His reference could not have been clearer.

These are the voices of the Jesus I've come to know. His strong teaching on "love your enemies" is the only one that makes sense for confronting the violence and hatreds of our world today, where weapons of destruction are technologically perfected and available to people in all countries. Many beside myself have written that we now face the final choice, nonviolence or nonexistence. The choice has become ever more crucial today for not only are we in a nuclear age, but it is increasingly one in which brothers hate brothers so deeply that they engage in "ethnic cleansing," the euphemism for genocide. While Jesus has spoken through voices like Ghandi's, Martin Luther King, Archbishop Romero, and recent Popes, the message of nonviolence remains smothered by the noise and destruction of violence.

Jesus' way holds the key to survival. He spoke continuously of compassion, mercy, forgiveness, and overcoming hate with love. The world talks of vengeance and retaliation. Everything Jesus was about could be said to be a contradiction to the world. Jesus never backed down, even to the death. He had to show us how to make the world right and this could only be done when we, the children of his Father, end conflict, hate, vengeance, and war, and become loving people who seek forgiveness and peace.

While Jesus is unique in his origins and mission, his urgings for peace are a universal call found in many religions. Buddhism teaches that true happiness requires that we live in peace with our fellow man. Confucianism says that "peace and love should reign throughout the world" and that "The Most High God seeks peace among his people." Hinduism maintains that "God is a God of peace and desires peace for all people." Islam offers the same message, that God will guide people to peace "if they will heed him." Then he will "lead them from the darkness of war to the light of peace."

Peace comes up in the Psalms, Proverbs, Ecclesiastes, and Isaiah, and the bottom line here is that the peaceful life offers the greatest opportunity for happiness and prosperity, maintaining that God commands peace and urges all his followers to work for peace. Jainism says strongly that "The enlightened will make peace the foundation of their lives. All men should live in peace with their fellows. This is the Lord's desire." And Taoism follows suit with "The good ruler seeks peace and not war, and he rules by persuasion rather than by force."

And yet, in this early twenty-first century, we hear constant talk of "religious wars!"

Jesus lived to bring us this message, that our Father wants us to make this a world without hatred, greed, and egos that always want to "even the score." He showed us the work we have to do to make this a world of peace, not war. We had better not delay any longer. Even General Douglas MacArthur, who served in two World Wars, and Korea, when he was seventy-one, warned that time was running out:

> With the scientific methods which have made mass destruction reach appalling proportions, war has ceased to be a sort of roll-of-the-dice. . . . The integration of the world . . . has outlawed the very basic concepts upon which war was used as a final word to settle international disputes. . . . If you have another war . . . only those will be happy that are dead.
>
> Sooner or later, if civilization is to survive . . . war must go.

8

Jesus Gave a Non-Negotiable Command—

To Forgive

Forgiveness is the love that reaches into the dark spaces of our failings and brokenness, picks us up, and holds us tenderly until we are healed.

—ALLAN WEINERT, CSsR

On a December Sunday in the late 1970s, my son Peter and I had come back from a quick trip to Albany to visit relatives. The sense of something being wrong hit us as soon as we saw the broken windows in the garage. When we opened the door and turned on the lights, we were dismayed as we saw the house in disarray and in a shambles. It was clear that the house had been broken into.

As we went through the house, we were impressed with the thoroughness of the thieves. Every drawer in each room had been pulled out, its contents scrambled, with items on the floors. Pictures on the walls had been disturbed, obviously by the invaders in search of a wall safe.

Little by little we counted up the missing items. Gone were the stereo, the lamps, grocery money left in a kitchen cabinet, Peter's coin collection saved over many years, my son Frank's two guitars, my accordion, virtually anything that looked like jewelry from the drawers in my and my daughters' bedrooms, my Nikkormat camera and two lenses, a ten-speed bike, many smaller items like a shell, vase, metal sculptures, a glass Madonna, etc., and a few irreplaceables.

There were other losses that hurt in a particular way, like not finding a special gift my son Paul had given me three Christmases earlier, a miniature grandfather clock. At that time, Paul was just out of college and unemployed. Yet he managed to scrape together some money and he found a gift he knew I'd love in a second hand thrift shop. That clock, so precious to me, would bring the thieves a five dollar bill at most from whoever they sold to.

Then, I had a gold watch with an inscription. It was as gift given to me by my co-workers at the newspaper when I left after working there for eleven years. I didn't know how thieves could peddle an inscribed watch for much, if anything, but I was left with a terrible void. That watch, a gift from great friends, had a special meaning for me.

They took another item I knew was irreplaceable, again a Christmas gift from my son Paul. At a coin auction he had found a rare three-dimensional 1912 American coin. It was beautiful and I had it made into a pendant to wear on special occasions. His thoughtfulness was touching and we had agreed that I would wear his gift and leave it for him to have forever as a remembrance of me and this Christmas after my death. The thieves intruded upon that intimate pact between myself and my son.

I had a few moments of real panic when I saw that my picture of Jesus beckoning me was not on my bedroom wall. Fortunately the thieves saw no value in it, for they had thrown it on the floor, tossed aside with some of my books and clothing. With a prayer of thanks, I put it back on the wall.

By the time Peter and I did a tally of the rip-off, I found myself overwhelmed with a sense of outrage. The terrible invasion of privacy angered me. The thought of people entering my home and putting their hands on my personal belongings, even my lingerie, filled me with revulsion. I had never thought too much about what kind of crime thievery really was. It never struck me as being particularly heinous since thieves take things, and things are replaceable.

That day, I learned that I was wrong. Thieves also violate you. They force their way into your personal realm; care nothing at all about your right to keep your personal world intact; and give you a legacy of uneasiness and distrust. I learned that thieves are people who leave disorder and victims, and some empty spaces that may never be filled again. Still, I looked upon this as a manageable disruption. No one was hurt; it was not really a life and death matter.

The thieves were nameless and faceless. It crossed my mind that I was supposed to forgive them, whatever that meant, since I was always preaching forgiveness, citing my Lord Jesus. But in truth, I didn't think of them as people, only ghostly shadows who had disrupted the order of my life. I spent no time or energy on forgiving these ghosts, because every time I thought of them— which was every time I discovered yet another missing item—I felt myself going into yet another rage!

I found that this new assault on my belongings and my life kept bringing back recollections of other times when I endured loss at the hands of destructive people. A year or two earlier I had come home from work and gone into the backyard to enjoy a few moments with the grass, the trees, and my tiny garden, only to find everything trampled on and destroyed. Branches from a small pear tree I had planted five years earlier were all over the ground. This was the first year the tree had actually borne fruit and I had counted forty pears on it. Not a pear was in sight. I figured that someone, maybe two or three, had wanted the still unripe pears and in stealing them were quite unconcerned about their vandalism. I wasn't in a forgiving mood, so it was just as well that I didn't know who did this.

Some years earlier when my son John was about ten years old, he had bought some Japanese wind chimes for me with a few dollars he had saved from his paper route. I loved that gift from my young son, and hung the chimes over a ledge above the front door. Within a week, a six-foot-two fifteen-year-old son of a neighbor had yanked them down, obviously enjoying the painful sound as he shook them violently until the parts were undone. I heard the cacophony from my kitchen and rushed out too late to stop the damage. The boy, embarrassed at being confronted, apologized, saying he thought they were junk. I don't remember what I said to him, but I know I didn't say, "I forgive you."

By that time my life had been a truly difficult one, not only personally, but professionally, too, in meeting many people who had lived through or were suffering injustices. I felt tremendous empathy for anyone who had suffered a severe loss, who was in pain, who had been hurt by another. I could give Mickey Mouse advice, talk about the need to forgive so one could get on with life, but in all honesty, I could relate better to my young sister Loretta, who had been dealing with recurring setbacks and had a mantra—"There's no justice!"

I kept meeting people over and over again in my life who went to church and said they believed in the teachings of Jesus, but then would go on to mention a few exceptions, mainly the one on forgiveness. To "love enemies" and forgive people because "they don't know what they're doing" made no sense when someone was insulted, hurt, defiled, or victimized in any way by another. The majority position seemed to be in agreement with what a British psychiatrist named Ian Suttie wrote back in the 1930s: "The last prayer, 'forgive them for they know not what they do,' seems to imply that forgiveness is not a condescension to an unworthy object, but a recognition that evil is merely error, not to be met by retributive error. The whole of this story illustrates non-retaliation—even non-resistance—to the very utmost limit." Well, if that was what Jesus was really saying, then why should any of us followers take it seriously?

Still, I was finding that the majority position always came out that if somebody hurts you, takes something from you, makes you a victim, then you don't have to take what Jesus said about forgiveness literally. You have a right to punch back. Growing up in an Italian-American milieu, I had become familiar with this. I often heard my Italian *paisans* use the word *sistemare*. One day I asked my mother what that meant. She got that strange, authoritative look on her face that used to give me chills, and said, with no explanation, "That means 'to even the score.'" No explanation was needed. I already knew about retribution, retaliation, and vengeance. It was on the front pages of the papers every day, and, sadly, in the neighborhoods. Years later I had pinned a quote from Goethe on my bedroom wall when I was in college to keep reminding me we were supposed to find a better way to deal with sins against us: "How could man live at all if he did not give absolution every night to himself and all his brothers?" But in all honesty, years later I knew I had never even come close to that ideal, which Jesus came to tell us had its origins in eternity.

The robbery had occurred as I had planned to prepare for Christmas. Now, as I was repairing the damage and shopping to replace missing essentials, the anger would surge up in me. I didn't like being in that place. I wanted to get over my very real feelings of anger, especially before all my kids would be home for the great holiday. I happened to turn on the TV, and a movie was coming on, *A Christmas Carol*. I thought I'd be bored if I watched it, because the story was so very familiar. Yet, I had always admired the wisdom Charles Dickens had in creating his tale. He dealt with the two ultimate themes—death and life—and with a human failing—greed, and the love of money which so easily carries one to the extreme of crowding out all the other things in life. This night, I felt a great admiration for Bob Cratchit, who was abused by Scrooge, but apparently was always a forgiving man. Maybe I could learn something from him, I felt. So, with thieves on my mind, I sat down and watched the movie.

As I could see the greedy Scrooge, the loveless man who exercises his power over his employee, Bob Cratchit, bleeding every ounce of labor from him to protect and increase his own wealth, I felt more anger, justifying the mood I was in. But suddenly that changed, thanks to Bob Cratchit, a man who so loves his family that he accepts the way his boss exploits him so as to keep his job and support those who are dependent on him. He also bears a cross, knowing he cannot provide the medical care needed by his son Tiny Tim, who is thereby doomed, facing an early death.

I was feeling very unforgiving of Scrooge, until I realized that Tiny Tim isn't the only one facing death. So is Scrooge, and herein lies the genius of Dickens. With his gift of being an imaginative storyteller, he creates an eerie setting that forces Scrooge to face his own evil and the doomed death this will lead him to. It is a bleak destiny for a man who has lived for money and exploited people for his own gain. Then, he is also forced to see the unjust death of a child, one that he might have prevented.

It seems a bit strange that a Christmas story deals with death, when Christmas is a time of birth, but Dickens clearly knew what he was trying to get across. By undergoing his symbolic death, Scrooge realizes how he has lost his life and he asks forgiveness and another chance—for a new life. It is a wish that is granted to him.

That night Dickens's story was just what I needed to jolt me out of my anger. I saw this as a tale of life renewed, in the rebirth of Scrooge and the saving of Tiny Tim. But it was also a reminder that people can have a second chance, that they can change for the better, that evil can be transformed into benevolence if one asks for forgiveness—witness Scrooge—and that love can be the avenue of new hope for renewed life—witness Tiny Tim.

At the end of the movie the announcer said something like Dickens hoped that his story would "pleasantly haunt the lives of his audiences." I felt he wanted to do much more, to show us how the bad Scrooge in all of us must die so that we can be reborn into goodness and life. This wasn't an original thought. I had heard it expressed as "a seed dying" from the teachings of Jesus, precisely so that we could emerge a new and better person, someone like himself. And a key element of it all was, precisely, forgiveness—Scrooge asking for it, but Tiny Tim and his family freely giving it.

I think what I really learned that night was that I hadn't turned the TV on by accident. I'm not saying God-made-me-do-it, but only that I needed to get spiritually into a better place and *A Christmas Carol,* which was "coincidentally" on the tube, helped me get there. I had been unprepared for the new emotions I felt after that brush with thieves. The fury focused on the thieves that would rise up unexpectedly in me, violated my comfortable, "good" self-image and left me at times facing a naked stranger. I could still chuckle when a friend would say "A conservative is a liberal who's been mugged." Only now I was tempted to believe that, which was completely out of character for me. I didn't want to stay there.

After the robbery I had wondered if a thief, mugger, or murderer ever thinks about their victims. A Catholic chaplain at a county jail told me, "Rarely. Most of them don't deal with victims as persons. The victim has something they want and so they take it."

He went on to talk about the criminal justice system itself, which is designed to keep the criminal separated from his victim and thus removed from any reminders of the consequences of his crime. "When you consider crime, punishment, retribution, and rehabilitation, you see very clearly that the system makes the criminal responsible not to the victim, but to society. And impersonalism is built into the system. Once he's caught, he becomes identified with categories— burglary, rape, assault and such. He almost never has to confront a person he has impoverished or maimed or the families of someone he murdered. Thus, he doesn't have to feel. If he should express remorse, it's usually only sorrow that he got caught," the chaplain told me, expressing his opinion that the system was tragically flawed and needed serious reform.

"Doesn't this make it much harder for the victim, then, to forgive?" I asked him. He shrugged, and said, "That depends on the victim." He explained that if victims want to nourish their pain, hang on to their anger, and stay justified in hating someone who has hurt them, they may enjoy their self-pity, but they'll be immobilized. If a victim wants to be internally free, that person has to forgive the one who harmed them. There's no other way. And this is Jesus' way. He spoke like he was underlining his words.

So I forgave the thieves, as I had forgiven all the people of my past who had hurt me. It was not a hard thing to do. I had a good life. I had my children. I could even talk again eloquently about forgiveness, especially after I took a couple of them to see *Camelot*, about the idyllic kingdom of King Arthur that cracks when his wife Guinivere and his most trusted knight Lancelot fall in love.

I told them this story was a religion lesson straight from the teachings of Jesus, because it showed Arthur moving on from rage and anger to forgiveness. In the midst of the King's personal pain because of his beloved wife's betrayal, he suffers even more, knowing this illicit relationship will erode his life's work as symbolized in the Round Table—the initiation of a new order of chivalry and righteousness. But then, Arthur suddenly stops. The focus on himself changes. Instead, he thinks of Guinivere and Lancelot, asking poignantly, "But what of *their* pain?" He is able to understand that they, too, are in a trap they didn't ask for. Magnificently, he is able to find a compassion, forgiveness, and love for them greater than his love for himself. Back at the time of the Camelot film, sure of myself, I had no doubt that if I were confronted with such a betrayal, I would be forgiving, like King Arthur.

But that was before I lost a son, at the hands of a murderer. Then, in the space of a phone call, I had to struggle with whether forgiveness, was possible, whether it ever made sense, and even whether it was the right thing. Considering the state of my soul, forgiveness could never be defined in any of the self-sure ways that I had thought of it before. I would have nightmares imagining what had happened in the bedroom where my son John and his wife Nancy were sleeping at 2:00 a.m. on August 12, 1993. I would break out in a sweat thinking of the violence, the sin, that happened that night, when an eighteen-year-old named Joseph Shadow Clark slid through a basement window into their home, stealthily went up the stairs to the bedroom where they were sleeping, and shot them to death with his nine millimeter semiautomatic gun. The word "forgiveness" never crossed my mind, and if it had, I would have written it off as a nonsensical set of letters from another dimension. I was no King Arthur!

Shadow Clark was the son of the couple from whom John and Nancy had recently purchased their home in Montana, the state they wanted to live in for its rustic and natural beauty. As for why he killed them, I'll never really know. He said he used to dream about killing and then one day he did it. He did want to know what it felt like to kill. He did insist he was a good kid and a really good student who never did anything bad, until this, and so he shouldn't be judged too harshly. He was a Fundamentalist Christian, who had gone to Christian schools and was in the Assembly of God church choir. What would bring a Christian boy to cold-heartedly assassinate two beautiful people?

I struggled with that question and realized very soon that there was only one path that could help me survive—to put my life solidly in the hands of my God. My children helped me, as we struggled together to find our souls, so damaged by this horror. We quickly came to one decision. We did not want more killing. We had always been dismayed at the death penalty, which Shadow Clark was facing. We made the decision to write to the judge and tell him that as the victims' family, we would seek life in prison for him, not death. In the end, he was given life, with the possibility of parole when he is sixty.

I didn't want Shadow Clark executed, but did that mean I had forgiven him? That question seared my soul as I sought Jesus' help, begging him to help me understand what he meant by "love your enemies" when the enemy had murdered your loved ones. I know Jesus had asked forgiveness for those who were killing him, and I felt I perhaps could do the same, if the physical injury had been done to *me*. But that boy had killed my children! That was different. That was unforgivable!

I didn't know then, when the wound was so raw, that forgiveness takes time, and that I had never really understood what forgiveness meant. I thought I could eventually deal with this, forgive Shadow Clark, and be done with it. Because I wanted to speed things up, I kept going back to the gospels, hoping for clarification on forgiveness, which seemed to be a non-negotiable teaching on the part of Jesus. I wondered how confused Peter must have been with Jesus' answer when he asked him how often he had to forgive someone who sinned against him, seven times? No, Peter, you've got it wrong. You forgive seventy times seven times. What in the name of heaven could he have meant by that?

I begged for clarification and guidance and one day I understood. This wasn't a numbers game that Jesus was playing. He was telling Peter that forgiveness is not a one time thing, or a seventy times thing. Forgiveness was something intrinsic to our breathing. Forgiveness had to be a continuous way of life. Forgiveness had to be always present tense, for it was never done. I was never going to be able to say, "I *forgave* Shadow Clark." For this to be truth, I would have to say for the rest of my life, "I *forgive* Shadow Clark." I had no idea how I could continually reaffirm forgiveness, especially when I was so shattered, so unsure of who I would now become. I then knew only one thing for sure—my pain was permanent, it would always be with me.

Unexpectedly, I got a call from my daughter Mary. She had read something about a man named Bill Pelke, who belonged to a group called Murder Victims Families for Reconcilation and led marches against the death penalty that were called the Journey of Hope. She thought it would help me to get in touch with him. I did and I learned that there were many people like myself who had survived the murder of family members and did not want revenge. Bill, who from that call became a lifelong friend, put me in touch with his group of people who, like ourselves, sought mercy and forgiveness for the killers of their loved ones.

I heard their stories but none touched me as deeply as the one lived by Gayle Blount, whose nineteen-year-old daughter Catherine had been stabbed to death by a man in 1980. After a period of grief and rage, pain and sadness, this mother, working with spiritual teachers, moved beyond hatred and vengeance. She began writing to the murderer, saying honestly, "This does not mean that I think you are innocent or that you are blameless for what happened." It was what she then said that made an imprint in my heart: "What I learned is this: You are a divine child of God. You carry the Christ-consciousness within you. You are surrounded by God's love even as you sit in your cell."

I cried my eyes out. She made me understand in a new way what Jesus meant by forgiveness, and why it must be a way of life, a way to live continuously. Now I could see that the minute we say "no" to forgiveness, we are gouging Christ out of our lives, and from that resulting emptiness of soul, we have nothing to give another.

Gayle Blount went beyond letter writing. She became involved with the lives of inmates on death row in San Quentin. Again I could see the Christ in her, seeking out the Christ who was in prison, visiting him. I had no specific plan to do the same, until I received an unexpected phone call from a man who was involved with REC, Residents Encounter Christ, a retreat program for inmates at Green Haven, a maximum security prison in New York state. He had read some of my anti–death penalty columns and invited me to give the "Peace Talk" at the closing Mass of the retreat to the inmates. I took this as a sign that I was supposed to meet Christ behind the bars. I had no way of knowing then how many prisoners, men and women, I would meet, talk to, and write to from that first encounter and ever since.

As I studied the criminal justice system and the prison industry, I became appalled at the emphasis on punishment and the lack of concern I sometimes encountered about the question of innocence. We have proof now that many people on death row are innocent, mainly because of DNA testing which validates that innocence. More than 110 prisoners have to date been released from death row, found innocent. Of course, there is no way ever of knowing how many people who were innocent have been executed in the United States, the only western nation to still use killing for punishment. Former Illinois Governor George Ryan, when he declared a moratorium on executions in his state in 2000, after thirteen men on death row were found innocent, spoke the truth, that he would not want to be a party to "the ultimate nightmare—the state's taking of an innocent life."

An even more chilling problem is that for many in the criminal justice system, innocence is "irrelevant," proved once more by an encounter in 2003 between a judge and an assistant state attorney general in Missouri. A death row inmate, claiming new evidence, was trying to have his conviction reopened. The prosecutor was trying to block this. "Are you suggesting that even if we find Mr. Amrine is actually innocent he should be executed?" asked Judge Laura Denvir Stith.

Frank A. Jung, the prosecutor, replied, "That's correct, your honor."

As the story went on, the justification for not allowing new evidence brought in that might prove the innocence of a person on death row is quite practical, because as Jeremiah W. Nixon, Missouri's attorney general, explained, "There must be a time when cases can be closed." In other words, what's important here is the clock. If time runs out because of some arbitrary deadline blocking new evidence—even DNA proof that a convicted person did not do that crime—well, that's just tough luck.

Acknowledged innocence should matter, not be ignored to accommodate a deadline or death for the convenience of the state!

I credit Robert J. Zani, a Catholic prisoner writing to me from his solitary cell in Texas, a state that keeps its death house busy, for helping me see how "acknowledged innocence" is given little, if any, real attention in death penalty cases. "See what Jesus and John the Baptist were up against?" he comments.

Robert maintains that ending the death penalty hinges on the innocence issue. "Innocence is no longer relevant in the criminal justice system because it is no longer relevant in the hearts and minds of Americans. The question of innocence is pivotal in seeking any reforms of the criminal justice system because when it's a death penalty case, a mistake is fatal." Robert quotes law professors Fred Bennett of Catholic University and Alan Raphael of Loyola University, who said, "Death penalty opponents will not be successful until the focus is placed on innocent people." I think Jesus would be behind that statement.

My ministry with prisoners goes on. Remembering what the chaplain told me back in the 1970s about the "impersonalism" that gets solidified by the criminal justice system, I wanted to test that. What I've found is

Jesus Gave a Non-Negotiable Command—To Forgive

that many prisoners rise above the system. They welcome contact with "victims," people like myself who have had to deal with terrible crime. I have had many encounters with prisoners, dialoging with them about the effect of crime on a family. Many have asked me to forgive them, in the name of the person they hurt, and I have seen tears in the eyes of many when I say, "I forgive you." I answer the uncountable number of letters they have sent me, finding great spirituality, artistry, and humility in them.

The work I do with prisoners fits in with the process that is known as "restorative justice," a most active form of forgiveness, which seeks to bring the guilty and the harmed together so that healing, and not punishment, can take place. Our criminal justice system is based on "retributive justice," accent on punishment, the "eye for an eye" variety. I ask myself which one would Jesus choose and I don't have to wait for an answer.

Some individuals I know who believe in retributive justice have told me that people have taken "this forgiveness thing" too far. I have a love story that says differently, one between a father incarcerated for twenty years in a maximum security prison, and a daughter, now twenty-something, who was a toddler when her father was sent away. I came to know April Grosso several years ago when her father, Charlie, introduced us at the annual Holy Name Society picnic at Green Haven prison in New York state, his "home." She is beautiful, with expressive blue-grey eyes that sometimes show a hint of a tear when she talks of her father, who had never been arrested and had no record at all when he was taken from their home, charged with a double homicide that had occurred nine months earlier, on the word of a jailhouse informant.

She never abandoned her father, visiting him from her childhood when her mother and relatives would bring her to the prison. I'll never forget how touched I was when April told me, "I would never let the criminal justice system come between me and my father."

When April became pregnant, she told her father she had found out that her baby would be a boy. Charlie, who talks and writes to me often, sent me a letter, saying:

Last night I was lying on my bed thinking about my up and coming grandson's name. . . . The name that came to mind was "Justin". I then wrote down "Justin Edward"—Eddie was my wife's brother who died before we got married, hit by a car—and mailed it out this morning.

Now tonight I got a letter from April, and in it she also wrote a name down, "Justus." I couldn't believe my eyes!

I knew why April picked that name. When she was younger, around sixteen, she wrote me and said, "Dad, there is no justice, but there will always be *Just-Us*." I began putting a book together for her then that I titled "Just-Us." When she comes to visit on Saturday we will get a laugh because she will be all misty knowing that I wrote her "Justin," and she wrote "Justus" and our letters crossed in the mail.

I had never expected such a beautiful love story to come from a prison. I thank the Lord Jesus that I have seen and been a part of restorative justice in action.

I have been asked many times, sometimes with hostility, "How is forgiveness possible when someone kills those you love? Isn't it just weakness to forgive? Isn't that letting evildoers get away with their hurting actions?"

I let Jesus, bearing the name of Pope John Paul II, answer these questions. "Forgiveness is above all a personal choice, a decision of the heart to go against the natural instinct to pay back evil with evil. . . . Forgiveness may seem like weakness, but it demands great spiritual strength and moral courage, both in granting it and accepting it." And he underscores, "What sufferings are inflicted on humanity because of the failure to reconcile!"

Philosophers and poets both have known this truth. Baruch Spinoza, a Dutch philosopher in the seventeenth century, would say, "Hatred can never do any good. . . . He who lives under the guidance of reason endeavors as much as possible to repay his fellow's hatred, rage, contempt, etc., with love and nobleness." And William Blake, the eighteenth-century English poet, affirmed the same—

Injury, the Lord heals, but Vengeance cannot be healed.

9

The Challenge of Keeping Jesus

Ever Alive on Earth

Here on earth God's work

must truly be our own.

—JOHN F. KENNEDY

Back in the early 1970s I was assigned to cover a talk being given by the Dutch priest psychologist, Father Adrian Van Kamm, who was to speak on how to understand and deal with midlife crisis. His audience was mainly priests and counseling professionals, with the talk being held under the auspices of a hospital. Judging from the crowd that showed up, and observing that they all looked older than I was, the journalist in me jotted down, "hot topic!"

Well, it was, and this very personable priest kept everyone's attention, especially when he talked about how it had become fashionable to think of age fifty as the "peak." Actually, he said, that's a time in which we have a choice—to begin passage to a deeper life, recognizing that the core of our lives is spiritual; or, to get locked into our desire to be functional, achieving, and powerful, refusing to accept normal decline as we get older, becoming more and more discontented as we enter old age.

Midlife crisis, he went on, begins with recognizable signs. You begin to feel a certain boredom that translates into a feeling of being trapped. There is a crisis of intimacy, a failure to sense a closeness in relating to others. You begin to identify persons and things in your life with this overall dismalness and blame your spouse, your job, or something else for your negative feelings. You feel physically let down and professionally threatened as younger people come along appearing to do most everything better than you can. You start to get depressed and feel anxious, though you can't put your finger on why you should feel this way. You also have strange feelings of false guilt and shame.

This is the onslaught of midlife crisis, and it can be explained, said Father Van Kaam—to everyone's relief! What is happening to you is that you are experiencing strong awareness of your own finiteness, of your limitations and your losses. Looking backwards, you are aware of all your unachieved hopes, all your unresolved problems; looking forward, you see the end of your life; and so, internally, there is a cry—a mourning for what you are losing.

At the same time, the negative feelings can bring you to a new threshold, where the spirit announces itself and forces you to ask in a critical way, What is my life all about? This is the crucial question—for if our response is to deny what is happening to us, to repress our mourning, to escape by any means possible, to stagnate by refusing to go deeper into our spiritual core to seek the meaning of life, then the midlife crisis can deform us. The result is bitterness, where you become an old person with no graciousness, only frustration, who labels life itself a disappointment.

On the other hand, if you make a value shift now, to seek and express a real, generous caring for society and those around you, to open yourself to the holy and the sacred, to be no longer frantic about achieving, to enjoy moments of aloneness and solitude, then you become "*a blessed presence to others*" in your old age.

Father Van Kaam brought out quite beautifully that while decline begins to set in sometime after midlife and puts our functional, vital life on the beginning of a descent, there is one area in which we can soar and grow in strength—the spiritual. The midlife crisis gives us the chance to make the most important breakthrough a person can make. It put us on the rim of a new function—the spiritual—and gives us the choice of turning to more inward values, to reconciliation, and to the discovery of the mystery of our life direction.

I was impressed with everything he said, but one expression took root in my soul. I was mesmerized by his observation that some people grow older and become "a blessed presence to others." I felt I had known many such people. But the more I thought, the more I realized that I knew a lot of people who fit that description and they weren't anywhere near old age! These were the people I had worked with in churches, in schools, in prison ministry, in interracial justice, in human rights, and in nursing homes, to name a sampling. They were the people I had met who took the words of Jesus in Matthew 25 so seriously that I never doubted that Jesus was ever-alive on this earth. They believed as Chad Walsh, a man who constantly found Jesus being born "anew in the manger of my heart," wrote, more than a half century ago:

> Christ revealed that all need is his need. Any hungry baby is a hungry Christ child; any weary traveler is the traveler who walked many weary

miles to preach and minister; any man in pain anywhere is the nailed Christ. . . . Whoever suffers need, has the suffering Christ within him. Whoever gives food or drink or meets any other human need is serving the needy Christ.

At about the same time Chad Walsh, an educator and literary critic, was writing this, back in the 1940s, I had been somewhat vaguely introduced to this challenge of how we must keep Jesus alive by seeing him in every living person. This message, I later understood, was the meaning in the beckoning fingers of Jesus in that picture I "saw" first without my eyes.

By the time, so many years later, that I was sitting in that room, listening to Father Van Kaam, I had tried to recommit myself over and over to work as Jesus would want me to in this world, for my family, my church, and my community. I had done extensive Confraternity work, was working probono as a Human Rights Commissioner in Suffolk County, was employed as a community relations specialist at a university and working hard as a single mom to launch my six children well so they could one day find their tasks in this world. I hadn't thought much about the future, but it was that expression of Father Van Kaam's—"blessed presence to others"—that took root in my soul. I wrote it down, underlined it and noted, this is for everybody, this is how we keep Jesus alive in our world.

So many times since then, I have met or known people who have been a "blessed presence to others," being very unaware of how they present Jesus to others, like my father. My last memory of him is how he feebly waved to me from his bed at St. Peter's Hospital in Albany, New York, but with a broad and happy smile before he faded out to yet another intermittent oblivion. The tears rolled down my face as I saw him, turned to the side of his pillow, his arms slightly extended at his sides, his hands tied down, his legs straight, with his ankles crossed. He was Christ on the Cross—for seven weeks before he died on a December day in 1985.

Remarkably, in those weeks when his suffering was so very evident, he never complained, as he had never done in his life before. If he could be characterized in these last months, it was by his smiles, and his whispered thank-yous. Speaking for the eight of us, his children, my brother Richard sat at his bedside and thanked *him* for all he had done for us. He answered, "You don't have to thank me. It was my job."

I remember that last weekend I spent with him, when the hospital chaplain came in to speak to him. My father couldn't receive Holy Communion because his swallowing ability was gone, yet he kissed Father's hand as his own way of communicating. My father's smile and his faith in life were the blessings I had felt from a young age. As my brother Joe said, we saw our father become more and more childlike and innocent as his love for us became cleansed of complications, reverting to a state of pure simplicity. "In the end," Joe said, "we saw him leave the world with a gentility and sweetness that must have been very much like the way his own father saw him, as he entered the world."

If we doubted at all that our father was a blessed presence, all we had to do was speak to the hundreds who came to his wake. People from his past, who knew him as "Joe the butcher," spoke of his kindnesses to their families, especially recalling the food he always gave to the people who, as my brother Joe put it, "had too much month left at the end of their money."

And then there were people who had only met him after the heart attack that brought him to the hospital. When we saw two of his nurses, who deal with the sick and the dying every day, come to say a last good-bye to "Mister Joe, the man who always smiled," we knew again how special our father was. And when Mr. Kiernan, blind from a stroke, who had been in the bed next to my father for a week or so, came to the wake, we again felt awe. He asked for the eight of us by name, for while he couldn't see us, he'd gotten to know us by name and voice in the daily vigils we alternated to be with Dad.

My Dad was a blessed presence, more truly a Christ presence, to others in those last days and that is the greatest eulogy that could be spoken. I now wear the medal of the Blessed Mother on the chain that he brought from Italy and he wore all his life since he came to this country as a teenager, alone. And I bear the values he passed on to me early in life, especially those he said were most important—a clear conscience, a big family, a good education, and caring for others.

I had been struck, though, by my brother Joe's words, how our dad had become "more and more childlike and innocent *as his love for us became cleansed of complications.*" I understood what he meant, knowing that, though my father was a very good man, he had been a hard man, too, mostly in his younger and midlife years, overly strict, quick at times to raise his voice, and sometimes his hands, a frightening experience for children. Only once did I ever personally know his anger, Christmas of 1940.

I was twelve and just beginning to move out of the innocence of childhood and into a new awareness that the adult world held some painful mysteries I would rather not yet know about. My initiation had begun two months earlier when my little baby brother Jimmy almost died. I still remember my mother's screams when she went to nurse him and found him barely breathing. We had no phone back then, but luckily my sister Rosemary, then fourteen, and I were both home. She ran to a neighbor and phoned a doctor; I ran two blocks to the cathedral rectory and got Father Hogan, a warm, very human priest, to come with me quickly because Jimmy had not yet been baptized.

I can still see tiny Jimmy on a pillow on the dining room table, with Father Hogan quickly baptizing him, while the doctor, who had hastily arrived in that time when doctors still made house calls, gave him artificial respiration, squeezing his chest. Then the doctor put my mother and Jimmy into his car and drove to the hospital, with his left hand steering and his right hand continuing the artificial respiration. Joey was only five and he was crying. Rosemary was hugging him and I went into the bedroom to cry with a pain I had never before experienced, from facing the possibility that I might lose the little brother I so dearly loved.

Jimmy survived and I went to the cathedral every day to thank God. But by Christmas, I knew I had changed. I had started to notice subtle things, like my mother's irrational moods, my father's excessive smoking, my own nervousness from a new awareness that life can be so fragile. Christmas day itself was not pleasant. We had a houseful of cousins and my mother could not hide her resentment that she was stuck with a gigantic cooking chore. Jimmy was still frail and we kept him isolated from the crowd. Rosemary and I hovered over him like proverbial mother hens.

Unexpectedly, my cousin Mick's father-in-law came by. In those days, I didn't know what an alcoholic was. Now we were exposed to one for hours, on the most sacred day of Christmas. I noticed my father also drank too much that afternoon. About 4 o'clock, my father told me to go to the little store about a block away that was open on Christmas and get him some cigarettes. When I got there, the store was empty except for the owner's daughter. She handed me the cigarettes and as I was waiting to get change, the phone rang. It was, apparently, her boyfriend, and probably since I was a twelve-year-old kid, she had no qualms about keeping me waiting nearly twenty minutes before she got back to me with my father's change.

When I got back to the house, my father was waiting for me at the door. Almost shaking with rage because of my delay, which he assumed was my fault, he slapped me repeatedly, moving me through three rooms with his blows until I landed against the kitchen refrigerator. I was in a complete state of shock. I did not cry. I glared at him in disbelief and confusion and anger. It was the first time he had ever hit me, and I should add this was the last and only time. I blamed his explosion on the fact that he had had too much to drink, not knowing then about nicotine addiction, too. My hostility was also directed at the drunk man who had entered our home, uninvited, allowed to stay out of some kind of Italian "respect" my father had for his nephew's father-in-law.

About a half hour later, his remorse evident, my father tried to be nice to me, offering to take me to a movie. Haughtily, I said no. He had spoiled my Christmas. There was no way, no way, I would forgive him.

A few days later my mother told me that my father had gotten a telegram on Christmas Eve informing him that his mother—my grandmother who lived in Italy, a stranger to me—had died. That's why he had been so upset on Christmas, she said.

I went into the bathroom, locked the door, and started to cry. I felt I could understand his suffering, because only a few weeks earlier I had faced the possibility of Jimmy's death and been in agony over this. What pain my father must have felt knowing he would never again see his mother. My father had spoiled my Christmas, but now that meant nothing. All I could think of was how his own Christmas had been spoiled, and how all the days of his life, Christmas, the day to celebrate life, would trigger memories of death.

Every time I've been angry or hurt, every time I've wanted to scream at somebody, every time I've felt abused, I'm brought back to that Christmas day of 1940 for what I learned, not right away, of course, but over many years. It's that there is a hard side to the choices we make in our life's journey, precisely because we meet so many disruptions, confusions, tragedies, self-centered, mean, cruel people, unjust setbacks and losses, some deadly—all out of our control. Every step of the way, we're being formed by outside forces that hit us, darkening our vision, making us acknowledge a truth we abhor—that we are not in control of what happens to us in this world. This becomes tragic only if we then become cynical, not recognizing that we can always be in control of something much more important—of who we are becoming.

Yet, when life gets in the way, again and again, it sometimes blurs, sometimes blocks out, sometimes makes us forget how to be "a blessed presence to others," and so, Jesus fades away. How to bring him back can be a lost cause, a "no" decision, or a new rooting of grace, which is given to each of us at conception, beautifully described by the French writer Francois Mauriac as "God's footprints in a soul," a love that continues to exist no matter how we may reject it:

> God's footsteps are not effaced on our inner roads; we cover them with dust or mud, but they are not wiped out.

It was right after that Christmas of 1940 that I started working with my father in his meat market. He said there was only one rule, for his store and for life, "Antoinette, always be good to people." Much later in life I would realize that this was exactly what Jesus had preached, using perhaps the stronger word of "love one another." Few of us get up in the morning and say in words, "Today I am going to keep Jesus alive in this world." We get too distracted, putting on the coffee, getting the kids off to school, driving to work, focusing on the day's responsibilities. The only way we keep Jesus alive in this world is the way my father taught me—"be good to people"—four little words that could transform the universe, and make anyone who honored them "a blessed presence to others."

Dad's work of feeding others was carried on by my brother Joe, who had begun working with the Regional Food Bank when he heard about the problem of the hungry in the area. The Food Bank collected surplus and salvaged food, distributing it to more than 300 programs that fed the hungry in eastern New York. He put in countless hours, and people would ask him why he did this. He'd answer "I'm lucky to be around, so I thought I'd give something back." One time he smiled and explained, "I can't tell you how many times I've had the last rites." My brother has suffered from hairy cell leukemia, a rare illness he was stricken with after his Army days in Panama, acknowledged by the Veteran's Administration, when the Army was testing chemical and other weapons. He brought Jesus to the marketplace until his wife Jodi died of breast cancer, and his condition, ever more serious, forced him to stay home. Joe was and is ever "a blessed presence to others."

Jesus stays present in this world, not by wishing, only by hard work. But sometimes I fear that more effort goes into keeping Jesus popular than alive. Thirty years ago came a best-selling "man wanted" poster, showing a drawing of Jesus above the words, "He is still at large." Following this came the "Jesus Movement," so appealing to youth that they inked the message "try Jesus" on their sneakers. Then came the "Jesus freaks" and the "Campus Crusaders for Christ." Columbia University held a "Jesus Week," Jesus Christ wristwatches replaced Mickey Mouse watches, and then came the joke—buy the "Jesus-doll. It talks! Pull the strings and he recites the beatitudes." On the cultural beat, in this early seventies revival of Jesus, Broadway was beaming with its spectacular hit, *Jesus Christ Superstar*, and off-Broadway was bragging about its *Godspell*, then in its third successful year.

The Jesus Movement became so well-known that it caught the attention of the Vatican City daily newspaper, *L'Osservatore Romano*, which labeled this a genuine revival, "rediscovering the presence of God, the need for God." "Bob Dylan is selling millions of records singing the praise of the Lord," the article said, going on to note that "Hippies" had turned to St. Francis of Assisi and his way of life for inspiration.

I was fascinated by this Jesus revival at the time, but, like many religious leaders I interviewed back then, I wondered just exactly who was the Jesus attracting the young people? What was he being made into by all this attention? And what kind of behavior was resulting from making Jesus into a popular hero?

Some felt that young people were interpreting Jesus as being the one who did everything for them, wanting the complete surrender of their will, thus justifying them to be passive about their own role in working to make this a better world. As one youth worker was quoted to say, "We're given a life on earth and our interim here means conflict. It's the only way we grow. If the Jesus people retreat from conflict to reflect all the time, I would worry about their growth into a mature Christianity." Others felt the Jesus Movement was "intellectually hollow," all emotional feeling and no depth.

Personally, I was fascinated with all this Jesus attention. My children were of the age to be involved and we could talk and agree that youth were weighing the values then being offered to them as the way to all-happiness—money, power, sophistication, technology—and were finding these empty. All around them youth had found social disorder, violence, and dehumanization, and they wanted to say "no" to all this. They wanted to believe in something valid; only more than that, they wanted to believe in *someone*. And they found him, an authentic person of integrity—Jesus.

The fad-aspects of the Jesus Movement faded away, as did the "movement" itself. But I have known so many who discovered the real Jesus back then, the one who is a personal friend, who accepts them, forgives them, who is always there with them no matter where they are, who offers them life and joy. They keep Jesus alive, consciously or automatically, in the many ways they reach out to be "good to people." Today I meet many young people who wear a bracelet, saying, "What would Jesus do?" This is not a "fad." It's a strong step in making that choice for life, to be Jesus in this world.

I repeat again, I have met so many people, of all ages, who have been "a blessed presence to others," keeping Jesus alive in this world, and I know them for the great qualification they have in common—they radiate joy. Jesus, about to go to his execution, gave such an unbelievable gift to his followers, addressing the Father: "I speak these things in the world so that they may have my joy made complete in themselves." He gave them his joy! C. S. Lewis understood this, when he wrote:

> Dance and fame are frivolous, unimportant down here; for "down here" is not their natural place. Here they are a moment's rest from the life we were placed down here to live. But in this world, everything is upside down. . . . Joy is the serious business of heaven.

No wonder Jesus wanted to leave his joy here, to give those who would follow him a taste of heaven! So many know this, like St. John of the Cross, who said, "The soul of one who serves God always swims in joy, always keeps holiday and is always in the mood for singing." I think Jesus smiled a lot, and had a great sense of humor, especially when it came to paying taxes, and he sent his fishermen friends down to the water to grab a fish and pull a coin out of its mouth. Dante impressed me, too, when he writes, in his *Divine Comedy*, that after he had made the ascent from hell to purgatory and was close to the celestial sphere, he suddenly heard a sound he had not heard before. Stopping and listening, Dante wrote, "It sounded like the laughter of the universe."

I always remember a story that was sent to me for possible publication when I was the editor of *The Litchfield County Times* in Connecticut, written by Lydia Wolf, a woman who had lived in France in the World War II years. She told of a beautiful May day back in the 1940s when she was in a little town along the Loire, on a bicycle, and suddenly stopped to gaze at the exquisite arched doorway of an old stone church. In her words,

> I let my eyes travel idly up the arch, enjoying the charming small angel heads, some forty or fifty in all, which ran like a heavenly necklace around the edge. My gaze went from one somber little face to the next, all looking exactly alike, all so serious.
>
> I passed the apogee of the doorway framed thus and began my visual search down the right. Suddenly, unexpectedly, almost like an explosion, at about the fourth angel down, I stopped in disbelief—in disbelief and joy. The little face looking down at me down the centuries was different from all the others. It was smiling happily and joyously at all the world!
>
> There was just this one glorious exception. How did it come about all those many years ago? Was this aberration ordered by the master in charge of building the church? No, no, not likely. More likely, he was busy elsewhere one day—and an artisan, working up there on the endless repetitive carvings, suddenly on just such a May afternoon decided that surely there was *one* of the heavenly faces who dared to smile, nay laugh. He created what he knew in his heart was true. . . . "

That, as C. S. Lewis said, "Joy is the serious business of heaven!"

The fact that after nearly a half century, and a disastrous war, Lydia could still be uplifted by relating to an artisan of another era who wanted to add a little joy to the world, was just another proof to me that heaven's power comes forth in joy and laughter. Her story reminded me of a fairy tale I used to read in my youthful days, about a woman who never laughed. She got married and couldn't have children. She was told, by I don't remember who, that she couldn't have any children until she laughed five times. The story goes on about how she learns to laugh and then the laughing woman becomes this beautiful woman, who now has new life. And because she *has* new life, she can now *give* new life, and so she is able to have children. I found it so fascinating that the key to having and giving new life in this tale is laughter. Indeed, laughter is the serious business of heaven.

The gospels may not point it out in detail, but I know Jesus laughed a lot, from how he spoke and what he did. We are told that he knew the Psalms well, and I can imagine one he really followed was Psalm 100:1-2, "Make a joyful noise to the Lord, all the lands! Serve the Lord with gladness! Come into his presence with singing!" I can imagine him walking down the dusty roads some days, singing and smiling.

We keep Jesus alive doing the same, being "a blessed presence to others" as he was. "Cana of Galilee," Feodor Dostoevsky recalled. "Ah, that sweet miracle! It was not men's grief, but their joy Christ visited. He worked his first miracle to help men's gladness."

10

A How-To-Live Scenario

That Made No Sense

God becomes as we are

that we may be as He is.

—WILLIAM BLAKE

I am an enthusiastic celebrator of Columbus Day each October when the holiday rolls in. It's an occasion for me to remember my roots and heritage with pride. For it was one of my *paisans*—my countryman Columbus—who made the first connection between the world that was known and the "new land."

But I wasn't always comfortable being born Italian-American, daughter of an immigrant from Calabria. In my childhood back in the 1930s, Italians were often looked at as being "different," if not "dullard." I was proud of my parents, yet, at a very young age, I came to feel the sting of being judged negatively for my roots. The first awareness I had that I was "Italian"—and that it wasn't so great a thing to be—came when I was in second grade, and my parents had enrolled me in the closest elementary parochial school, attended almost entirely by Irish and Dutch Catholic children. The girls wore uniforms, white middy blouses, with a sailor boy tie, over blue pleated skirts. The uniforms had to be bought at a store called Lerners.

Well, we were poor and couldn't afford the Lerners price. So my very creative mother made my uniform, using a pair of my grandfather's old black pants for the skirt. We had an assembly that first day of school, all of us lined up by grade one to eight, walking into the auditorium, passing for inspection in front of the Mother superior who was the principal. When this gigantic, black-habited woman saw me, she pulled me out of the line, marched me on stage before the whole school population and berated me for the incorrect uniform. Somehow she managed to correlate this with my being Italian, telling the whole eight grades that even if I was Italian and poor, I still had to have the right uniform.

I was, fortunately, spunky. I spoke up in defense of our poverty, bragging about how my mother was clever enough to make my uniform out of my grandfather's pants, and marched off the stage without a tear. But when I got home, I cried my eyes out for having been denigrated before the whole school because of my birthright and my family's economic status. I wasn't proud. I think I was really ashamed.

As I grew older, I got used to hearing Italians being called disparaging names, and I understood why these first-generation Italian-Americans stayed together. They had brought over with them from the homeland a belief that family is the only valid unit and found this was even more true for them here. Only among their own kind could they feel comfortable. While I loved the earthiness, the laughter, the noise, the music, the warmth, the food, the children, the church—the elements of Italian life transposed to America—the sense that something was wrong with me, that I was less than my "American" classmates, would be a feeling triggered all too often by some schoolmate's insensitivity.

Having felt "different" all too often, I could empathize with two new students who transferred to my high school in ninth grade. They were from St. Peter Claver's, the black parish in the city. This was the first time the school had accepted any black kids from there to be enrolled as students. I became friendly with one of the boys. One day in late December we stayed late after school, talking, mostly about what we'd be doing for Christmas since it was close to the holiday. But then, unexpectedly, he said something about feeling strange in this school, commenting that sometimes he prayed at night that he'd wake up white. Wanting to make him feel more comfortable, I confided to him that sometimes I prayed at night that I'd wake up blonde and Irish.

Just then, one of the nuns—unfortunately not one of the many beautiful Sisters who loved all of us—came upon us and the shock on her face was evident. She told me I wasn't supposed to be seen with "him." He apologized and said he wouldn't be around much longer because he wasn't going to come back for the second semester. I told him I was sorry, shook his hand and then obeyed Sister, who brought me back into her classroom where she severely lectured me about associating with "one of them." Even an Italian should know better, she said.

That was the turnaround for me. The vague "shame" I had felt for being Italian was transformed to anger, that some people considered others lesser human beings. I was fourteen and I knew then and there that I would never again pray to wake up Irish or anything other than what I am. But I felt a terrible hostility towards that nun. I was very familiar with the teachings of Jesus, and

I knew we were not supposed to get angry, that we should love our enemies and pray for those who persecute us, but that day I discovered I was no saint. I went to my cathedral to make a visit on my way home, as I always did, and I think I very boldly told Jesus I thought he had made a mistake. What he said didn't make sense, not when someone hurts you, the way that Sister had hurt that boy, and me, too.

It was much later that I was to learn I was not alone in struggling with the impossible teachings of Jesus, the ones that on the surface made no sense. I have long saved a paragraph from the writings of the French novelist Francois Mauriac, conscious of the radical character of Jesus' ethics:

> Charity is not enough, he demands the folly of charity; to hold out the other cheek, to leave the cloak to the thief who has already taken the tunic; to love those who hate us. Was he mad? Yes, in the eyes of men it is a state of madness which Christ asks and will obtain from his loved ones. . . . It is a life full of snares and perils where everything is done prudently but in love.

At age fifteen, of course, when Jesus beckoned to me, I did not know that he was inviting me to a life "of snares and perils." I had gotten a clue from that nun's treatment of me and my black classmate that there was a disconnect between the world and Jesus in how both viewed people—disdain and abuse versus love. Already I had decided I would one day find a way to help my black brothers so they would never again feel compelled to pray that they'd wake up white. I never could have predicted what this meant for the coming decades of my life, risking arrests, working with many black friends for equal rights for housing, jobs, education, medical care, unions, and putting a spotlight on the color bias in the criminal justice system. There were tears, too, clasping the hand of my friend and colleague, Ken Anderson, when a cross was burned on his lawn for the human rights work we wouldn't stop.

That day, I have to admit, was a tough one for someone like me, who was very good at preaching how we're supposed to love everybody, even our enemies, and do good to those who hate us, have power over us, and hurt people who we love. It was just another one of those times when all I could say to the Lord, was "Sorry, not today." I was back with my recurring struggle to accept Jesus' impossible teachings, getting some help only from others who saw the same problem, like Carlo Carretto, a Little Brother of Charles de Foucauld:

There will be moments when you come up against almost insurmountable difficulties in your efforts, however great they may be, to love your neighbor.

Difficulties may be caused by his sin, his unkindness or his superficiality. When this happens, remember that to know how to love, when we read nothing but evil, deceit and slovenliness in our brother's face, is beyond human powers—yet we are so deeply immersed in what is human. It is then that you have to "act as if" you loved him with the very love of Jesus dying on the cross. . . . It would be unreasonable to expect feelings of love from a heart smarting under the hurt of some pain received, or of anything worse.

I had begun to learn, in my teens, that hearing the gospels read in church and trying to live them were two rather distinct realities. The first was so comforting, so uplifting when you could kneel before the altar and feel holy, promising Jesus to be like him, to "see him" in everybody. The second was drudge work. I was immersed in this when I got my first summer paying job, right out of high school in 1945 at age sixteen, in a factory and I met Jenny.

Jenny was a classic case of the crazies. She was my supervisor and would be sweet one minute and a monster the next. My feelings toward her, in all honesty, never came close to love, wavering from confusion to rage. One day she came in shaky and got worse as the day went on. That day we got swamped with work and had to stay overtime. Suddenly, Jenny broke down. She started moaning that the boyfriend she had been living with left her. She wanted to go to confession but she wouldn't because she said God couldn't forgive her for her terrible sins. She had killed her babies in back room abortions and had gotten sterilized.

I was in shock, of course. I didn't know women did such things. How could you live with a man if you weren't married to him? How could a mother-to-be have an abortion? In my Italian-Catholic culture, such sins were about as obscene as could be imagined. Yet, I believed that if someone went to confession, sins were forgiven. So I tried to tell Jenny not to be afraid to go to confession. God would forgive her, hoping to calm her down. Her response, instead, was fury. Her tears turned to stone and the hate in her face terrified me.

I could never understand what happened next, but suddenly I stopped being afraid of her and found myself beginning to feel her pain—the torture of a person whose whole existence is a contradiction, who sees everyone else and the world itself as a condemning judge. I didn't know back then, at age fifteen, that I was meeting Christ that day. Only in reflection over the years to come, when Jenny still haunted me, could I understand that he was there that day with his challenge to me not to judge, but to understand and love those around us who are unlovable. Jesus wanted me to feel the compassion he felt and to learn to care about her and all the scowling Jennies I was to meet in the next decades of my life.

Yet, in the matter of Jenny, I felt for years that there was some unfinished business here between me and Jesus. I could never forget how she said she was going to go to hell for her terrible sins. Because at that time she was not yet ready to believe in God's forgiveness, I feared she might be right. But even at age sixteen, I had a problem with the concept of hell we were taught, that it was place created by God to keep bad people in eternal torment for refusing to live by heavenly commandments while they were on earth. It seemed a very long punishment for a very short time as flesh and blood people. But many a Sunday sermon went on about hell, so who was I to offer any contradictions?

That confusion did not go away, especially as I got older and realized how difficult and crazy life can get, how hurt we can be, how unfair societies often are. I had long quoted Matthew 25 as the perfect blueprint for how we meet Jesus and how we show love. But I would stop, really confused, at the last sentence, when Jesus tells the fate of those who don't show love: "And these will go away into eternal punishment, but the righteous into eternal life." With words like that, could I deny the existence of hell?

Strange sometimes where you get an answer, even when you're not exactly looking for it at that moment. I had begun to study Dante's *Divine Comedy*, focusing very much on his *Inferno* (hell), not expecting what I would learn. By the time Dante wrote this magnificent work, he had made a choice to be not a citizen of Italy, where he had been a victim of partisan strife and trumped up charges of bribery, but "a citizen of the Christian world." He became a champion of the belief that if human Will becomes perfectly in accord with the Will of God, then there would be return to order and righteousness in this world.

For Dante, humanity has only one destiny—heaven, where we will be tucked forever in the womb of God, united to God in perfect, radiant happiness for all eternity. Now what he expresses next really got my attention. He believes this destiny will be denied to humanity *only if we refuse to choose heaven by a deliberate act of our own free will.* Thus, the cornerstone of Dante's concept of morality and salvation is freedom of the will. Without this, morality would have no meaning, rewards and punishments would be impossible, and Divine justice would be a cruel, cosmic joke. People, Dante believes, have unlimited freedom to choose to be integrated with the eternal plan of salvation designed by God—or to say no.

For Dante, nothing can dominate a person if he or she chooses not to let it, and there are no valid excuses for anyone to choose sin over salvation, which rests in a good God who has not remained hidden but has revealed himself. In fact, for Dante, a person doesn't get what he or she deserves, but what each chooses, and this is the essential feature of Dante's hell—*his souls there still have the same preferences they had on earth.* They have not only chosen their punishment; they are continually re-choosing this condition.

As you start to read the *Inferno*, Dante's position, that free will is not negated even after death, becomes a fascinating study. It is amazing how the characters in hell have a compulsion to talk about themselves. Never is there the mention of repentance. There is reference to pain and pity, but never does anyone say, "I wish I had another chance; I would have done things differently."

These people were mired in their sins on earth; they had chosen to sink within themselves, to do anything, regardless of harm to self or others, if it gratified what was dearest to their deep self-desires. Thus, they had exiled themselves, placed themselves beyond the possibility of community or unity with God, until they were hopelessly sunk within the solid tomb of their own isolation, where they existed with what they wanted and chose—their sin.

They dammed themselves, because even grace—God's footsteps—cannot penetrate the self-built walls that isolate a soul. They have made their own hell and cast themselves there. Even Satan, when we get to the pit of Dante's "Hell," is isolated, encased in ice.

I read and reread Dante's *Inferno*, finally understanding what Jesus meant by eternal punishment, seeing so clearly that this was never God's making, but a choice that had come from humankind. God never made hell. What the Father created for us is a place in heaven. Our final destination is our own choice, never made in ignorance, only in defiant arrogance.

I did find something about hell that was harder to figure out. Why is it that so many of us have to endure perils and snares that plunge us at times here on earth into a place we can only call "a living hell?" I have interviewed so many people who have had their lives shattered by unendurable pain, both in soul and in body. I have been asked how can I still believe in God when he allowed two of my children to die? Was I in hell? Oh yes. Was it God's fault? No. It was a faulty brain in Peter's head that killed him; a gun in the hand of a teenager that killed John and Nancy.

One woman, in terrible agony over the unexpected death of her husband, would not accept my answer. She quoted Jesus, saying which of you parents, if your child asks for bread will give him a stone? She taunted me, "Didn't God, your Father, give you a stone?" I answered something like, "Maybe it really was bread. Maybe it only looked like a stone. Maybe it was just the 'bread' I needed." I knew I sounded somewhat idiotic, as I went on to try to explain that sometimes what Jesus said comes across like an impossible teaching. We all know fathers who give stones to their children when they beat them, abandon them, deny them the love each child deserves. But God isn't like that. What he gives us might look like stone, but it's really bread in disguise. We just haven't recognized it yet. Maybe we did get the bread, but past tense. God was the one who should get my eternal thanks for having given me two beautiful sons and a lovely daughter-in-law to love. That was, and still is, my answer. I got what is called "polite applause." It may be all I deserved, but it was the best I could do.

I was on weak territory the day I interviewed Roger Berlind, a Broadway producer who had brought some wonderful, award-winning productions to the New York stages, like "Amadeus," "Guys and Dolls," "Hamlet" and, "Proof." He said he had always wanted to be in show business, majoring in drama and music at Princeton. He joined the U.S. Army in 1952, assigned to counterintelligence in Germany. Needing a job after his Army days, he was invited by an old friend to join him and two other men in starting a small investment-banking and retail brokerage firm. He became, in the next fifteen years, one of a team of high-powered Wall Street entrepreneurs, whose company ended up as Shearson-American Express, bought out in 1981 for about $875 million, making a fortune for the original partners, and subsidizing the work Mr. Berlind always wanted to do—great Broadway shows.

While Mr. Berlind was talking to me, I felt an incredible gentleness about him, and an aura I could only describe as a kind of silence even as he was speaking. At one point, I stopped taking notes and said outright, "You're different from all the people I've ever interviewed." He nodded and said, "My wife and three of my children were killed in a plane crash." I was shaken. I had lost my Peter a year and a half earlier. I knew the pain of surviving the death of one loved one. How could he have survived losing four?

His wife, Helen, who he always called "Polky," his daughter Helen, twelve, and sons Peter, nine, and Clark, six, had been to Hattiesburg, Mississippi, for a two-week visit with Polky's mother. Two-year-old William had stayed home with Daddy. His family was on Eastern Flight 66 from New Orleans on June 24, 1975, when it crashed on landing at Kennedy Airport. It was, he acknowledged, a mega-tragedy that left him to deal with "craziness and rage" for nearly a year. The only thing that had kept him going was William, who was then a twenty-year-old Princeton student.

Quietly, I asked him if he had a faith to help sustain him. "There was nothing to learn from this," Mr. Berlind told me. "It was meaningless. If there is a Master Plan, I have a lot of problems with it." I told him about my Peter, and said that the only thing keeping me going was my faith that he is happy with God now, and that someday I'll understand why there has to be such pain in this lifetime. He said, "I don't believe that. If I had been in charge of making this universe, I'd have designed it differently."

I answered something like "We don't have all the data, so we don't know why existence is the way it is, with so much pain and suffering," and then I went on with the interview, to discover a man of deep compassion for others in pain. At one point, he commented, "I look at Somalia and Bangladesh and see people so much worse off than I have ever been. . . . Life doesn't fit into a neat pattern. There's a great deal of luck involved in where you start out and where you end up."

Just one month after this interview, I got the news that my son John and his wife Nancy had been murdered. I received a message of heartfelt, compassionate empathy from Roger Berlind. It was such a human outreach. I was convinced that when Jesus spoke of how giving food and drink to someone was giving it to him, he was telling us there is a universal connection between him and each one who shows compassion for another, regardless of what religion or nonreligion that good person belongs to. "Only compassion can teach a person what solidarity with other human beings means. Of such is the 'kingdom' of God," says Father Albert Nolan of South Africa.

I found as the years went on that I would sometimes rather cynically challenge Jesus on what he meant by some of his teachings, depending on where I was in my life. I liked the sound of his beautiful, "Come to me all ye who labor and are burdened and I will refresh you," but for decades I wrote this off as some kind of joke. As a single mother with the full parenting responsibilities, including financial, of launching six individuals into maturity, I was on a non-stop treadmill. Not only was there the shopping, cooking, cleaning, working, chauffeuring, listening—I could go on. There was the moonlighting to make more money, and the unexpected complications, like a kid suddenly getting sick. My children still comment on the sign I posted in the kitchen that I would point to as I came home from work—"The deadline for all complaints was yesterday." "Jesus," I would pray, "I'm burdened, refresh me!"

I thought he wasn't listening, but one day I realized it was me. I was the one who wasn't listening. That day came after most of my children were grown. My daughter Mary was with me and we both had work to do for our jobs. It was January, but an unusually balmy day that gave me a mid-winter spell of "spring fever." I wanted to clean closets, listen to good music, read a book, write letters. What I didn't want to do was my ordinary work—writing. I faced my deadlines as though they were enemies. I stretched in the warm weather. I wanted a break.

I decided to make tea for myself and my daughter, and we sat and talked and laughed, joking about how we were pretending, for a change, to be ladies of leisure.

We talked about how long it had been since each of us had taken a day to do "a little of this and a little of that." We concluded that the price we were paying for our busy lives was having to give up the "joy of puttering." "When did you last take a day to putter?" Mary and I asked each other, knowing what we really meant was, are we finding the essential time needed for reflection on what we are here for, what our lives are about, what makes life worth living? We talked about how both of us needed our jobs for income, but asked—who has been crowded out of our lives, friends, ourselves, God?

After we finished our tea, I took a walk around my house and breathed deep breaths. Slowly I realized this day was not an accident. It was a message from God. He was pulling a little surprise to get me to stop, look, and listen—to him. I shut down the treadmill for a day, puttered, felt human, and meditated on my maker and the blessings of my life.

Jesus' words came back to me, "Come to me all ye who labor and are burdened—and I will refresh you." It was a benediction I had not thought about for a long time—not until there was a spring day in winter, and I realized he wasn't giving us words, but rather, offering an oasis that is life-giving.

I have learned that it is so easy to be somewhat cynical about the how-to-live-right program we can glean from the gospels. So much of it is to be made fun of if it is looked at solely from the values of the world. But what Jesus was saying was not of this world. "He towers over history, and calls people to follow him in changing the world," says my former teacher, N. T. Wright.

> The point at issue was not that Jesus was offering forgiveness where the rabbis were offering self-help moralism. The point is that Jesus was offering the return from exile, the renewed covenant, the eschatological "forgiveness of

sins"—in other words, the kingdom of God. And he was offering this final eschatological blessing outside the official structures, to all the wrong people, and on his own authority. That was his real offence.

What Jesus was offering, in other words, was not a different religious system. It was a new world order, the end of Israel's long desolation, the true and final "forgiveness of sins," the inauguration of the kingdom of God.

Jesus completely recast all the common ideas of what holiness is. He wanted to have all people see everything as God sees it, and to know that God didn't make the world and then disappear. God cares for the individual to an extent far beyond anything we can imagine. Jesus had a goal, and it was to induce all people to base their whole life on God.

Some eighty-five years ago, T. R. Glover of Cambridge wrote:

He means us to go about things in God's way—forgiving our enemies, cherishing kind thoughts about those who hate us or despise us or use us badly, praying for them. This takes us right back into the common world, where we have to live in any case; and it is there that he means us to live with God—not in trance, but at work, in the family, in business, shop, and street, doing all the little things and the great things that God wants us to do, and glad to do them because we are his children and he is our Father.

God knows—that is what Jesus repeats, God cares; and God can do things; his hands are not tied by impotence. The knowledge of God is emphasized by Jesus... knows your hearts, knows your struggles, knows your worries, knows your worth; God knows all about you. There is nothing he cannot do, nothing he will not do, for his children. . . . Jesus lays quite an unexpected emphasis on sheer tenderness—on kindness to neighbor and stranger, the instinctive humanity that helps men, if it be only by the swift offer of a cup of cold water. . . .

He sees how quarrels injure life, and alienate a man from God. Hence comes the famous saying: "Resist not evil; but whosoever shall smite thee on thy right cheek, turn to him the other also." . . . The parable of the king and his debtor, painfully true to human nature, brings out the whole matter of our forgiveness of one another into the light; we are shown it from God's outlook.

St. Augustine asked the question, how far are we prepared to go with Jesus? If we say, "all the way," then it means moving continually into a world that is a contradiction to the old one we've always known, because it is his Father's world. The rules between the two worlds are so different. We are so much more familiar with the ways of the world we were born into, that when we are given the rules of the world we really belong to, some of them don't seem to make sense, at least not automatically.

Yet, if we follow where Jesus beckons, the prize is packaged beyond anything we can imagine, for now we are in God's divine territory, discovering, as the poet John Donne affirms, that—

"All divinity is love or wonder."

11

Faith—*Redefined by Jesus*

I want to proclaim the

good news by my life.

—PERE CHARLES DE FOUCAULD

Abuilding was supposed to go up in a Long Island town in the mid-1970s, one that would be a good place for helping many special people in need. It would be a center where physically handicapped people could learn skills enabling them to earn a modest living; where ex-drug addicts and ex-convicts could work while making the transition from an institution to the community; where a thrift shop would be set up providing some of them with needed jobs and generating income. It was also to be a "mission" of the nearby Catholic parish, providing a central meeting place for the conducting of church social and educational affairs.

That center was a dream of the St. Vincent de Paul Society on Long Island—but it was a dream that went sour.

In order to build the facility, the St. Vincent de Paul Society had to apply to have the five acres of land on which it would be built rezoned. To the surprise of the Society, when the news of the rezoning became public, all fury broke loose. The local residents, the majority of whom were parishioners of the local Catholic Church, became a massive block of opposition to the very idea that such a facility could be planned in their midst. The opposition rallied supporters in the hundreds. And so, after several months of teetering and tottering, the plan fell apart. The local town board rejected the rezoning application and the St. Vincent de Paul Society abandoned its plan to build what had become a "controversial" center.

What really happened? Why would people, particularly Catholics, the major opposing block, fight against the construction of a place that would help so many people in need of concern, job training, and paid employment, opportunities that might put them back into the mainstream flow of productive life?

That's a troubling question, hard to answer, because the ingredients causing mass hostility are always a complicated pot. The leaders of the opposition claimed they were being robbed of a birthright of sorts. That land was supposed to get a church built on it, they said, not a center to "rehabilitate" misfits. Residents of the area said they raised money about twenty years earlier to purchase the land and they donated it as a site for a church to their diocese, then the Diocese of Brooklyn. Shortly after that, the Long Island section of the diocese was split off to form the Rockville Centre Diocese, which determined that since the property was located only one mile from the existing Catholic Church, it didn't make sense to build another one so close.

At that time I interviewed the priest-chaplain of the Society's Dismas Committee, the group that provided help mainly to prisoners and ex-convicts. He saw the opposition as due mainly to fear, most of it irrational. He speculated, though, that maybe the Society had failed to prepare the community properly before trying to push through a rezoning for a center that was sure to be unpopular in the community.

"Nobody wants drug addicts, ex-convicts and retarded people in their neighborhood. People don't feel safe when 'different' ones get close enough to become their neighbors," said this priest. He emphasized that the Society, expecting hostility would erupt, should have come to the community in advance, telling the residents exactly what was being planned. "That might, at least, have dispelled some of the terrible rumors that went around and led eventually to where 800 people literally engulfed the members of the Town Board with their demand for a 'no' vote on the rezoning."

The residents claimed the complex would "change the complexion of the town." The president of the local Taxpayers Association stated the center would not "improve our community by busing former alcoholics here. And our town does not need charity."

The noise quieted down as soon as the residents won. I took notes as I did my reporting job, jotting down comments like "Now our neighborhood will be safe." "We don't need help from a *Christian* organization," underscoring Christian with a sneer. "Let those undesirables go somewhere else."

There was, of course, one conscience-pricking question to ask—WHERE?

On Sunday the Catholic church had unusually large numbers of people coming for Mass. I guess they were there to celebrate their victory, and probably their faith, as they understood it, a comfortable faith, where one believes in God, says prayers on occasion, expects that prayers should be answered according to their own format, and knows that "God helps those who help themselves."

Ah faith! If ever a word has been misunderstood, abused, manipulated, redefined to suit one's fancy, and too often discarded, it is *faith*.

How many times has someone who has suffered a great injustice, a tragedy, or has been hurt in some unexpected way been told they'll find comfort in their faith, for "God sends suffering to those he loves the most." Or, "The back was made for the burden." Or, "God never sends a trial too heavy for one to bear." These pious and unreasonable explanations for crises, sorrows, and tragedy are about as healing as pouring holy water on the situation. They also obscure the reality that some people do indeed have physical and mental breakdowns from their burdens, and that maybe some people are, in fact, undergoing a pain that could be labeled unjust.

The "God sends loved ones sufferings" explanation is an affront to the very meaning of faith. It is an explanation so very unfair to God. It makes him an arbitrary chooser of who is to suffer and how much, ignoring the role of nature, humans, and existence itself in perpetrating difficult events. It actually distorts faith, making this an act of accepting God's unreasonableness, arbitrariness, and other negatives—intrinsically contradictory qualities in a Creator—rather than an act of confidence that God wills to sustain us in getting through a pain which the human condition, our earthly milieu, has caused.

Simplistic platitudes about God make him the cause of our pain rather than the hope of our healing. I have met so many people in my adult years who told me they "lost" their faith, or gave it up, because they prayed for something and did not get the response they wanted. Part of the blame for this goes back to early religious instructions where children were told to pray to God for everything they needed or wanted. It becomes an old tape that keeps playing back when we get older. The problem with this simplistic instruction is that we aren't born with the gift of being able to discern just exactly what this means. So we pray for things and when we don't get them, just the way we ask for, we scream at God. We want him to be some kind of Santa Claus in the sky, or at least a cosmic bellhop, catering to our requests, and this isn't God, nor is it the meaning of faith.

We've got to let God be God and not reduce him to someone who carries out our requests and demands. If we do the latter, we doom our faith from the start, just as we doom any relationship where one party says to the other—make me comfortable, rich, beautiful, serve me as I want to be served.

When Jesus came to earth, the people then also had a confused faith. The people were bound by a legalistic interpretation of religion. "Sophistical interpretations and absurd traditions had caused the law to degenerate into a terrible slavery, imposed in the name of God," wrote Franciscan Father Leonardo Boff.

To the Pharisees, particularly observant to the letter of the law, Jesus fairly exploded: "You have made a fine art of setting aside God's commandments in the interests of keeping your traditions!"

Instead of furthering liberation, the law had become a prison with golden bars. Instead of being an aid to human beings in the encounter with their fellows and with God, the law shut them off from both, discriminating between those whom God loved and those whom God did not love, between the pure and the impure, between my neighbor whom I should love and my enemy whom I may hate. The Pharisees had a morbid conception of God. Their God no longer spoke to human beings. Their God had left them a Law.

Father Boff, one of the architects of liberation theology, underscores,

> Jesus tore away their disguise . . . He summons his hearers to an absolutely transcendent dimension. . . . He does not proclaim a particular political, economic, religious meaning—but an absolute, all-comprehending, all-transcending meaning. His watchword, his key concept, is charged with radical meaning: he proclaims the "reign of God."

> Jesus determinedly refuses to establish a reign of power. He is the servant, not the dominator, of every human creature. It is God's love, then, not God's power, that Jesus incarnates.

Thus, central to his mission was the essential need to redefine faith, which was, precisely, let God be God, know that God is there and that he loves you, and very important, think like God thinks. Faith no longer could be self-centered. Jesus said faith means to identify with the needs of those we love and ought to love, and with the world's misery. He said, "Ask and you shall receive," but know what you're asking for, know that God has better things to give you than food and clothing alone. Clearly he was telling us that faith could never be an appendage; it is our life blood. Above all, faith means to see everything as God does, which means with the eyes of love, and a heart of joy.

Jesus redefined faith to let all know there is no meanness in God, no harsh judgment, rather, deep compassion. God loves us so much that he numbers the very hairs of our head, Jesus said, to emphasize the importance God gives to each person conceived.

Back in 1949, Fulton Oursler, a convert to Catholicism, wrote a book called *The Greatest Story Ever Told*, and he elaborated on the further ways God had made us unique:

Yes, "the very hairs of your head are all numbered." Thus, Jesus emphasized the uniqueness of the individual, and they loved it, though little comprehending the literal import of his words. But two thousand years later, in the laboratories of modern criminologists, the spectrograph and spectrophotometer show us that the hair on every mortal head is different from all others; and more, that each individual hair is "numbered," is different from any other hair on the same head! Not only are there no two thumbs or fingerprints alike in all humanity, but even the lines and whorls and loops and corrugations on the hoofs of cows and bulls and the feet of dogs and cats are all unparalleled. It is science today that shows individuality to be of persistent uniqueness in God's world, just as Jesus taught it.

Science was to learn that not one man's sweat was like another's; you could break it down into its chemical elements, and find an infinite diversity in mere drops of perspiration. . . . Every part of me and you is intrinsically and unmistakably you and me; the combination and proportions of your phosphorous and calcium and all the rest of you are unique.

Since then science has proven so much more about our individuality, notably how we are identified by our DNA.

That immense importance of your uniqueness, and mine, your individuality, your immortal soul was what Jesus was trying to bring home to the people,

wrote Mr. Oursler.

It's no wonder then that Jesus would hold us to very high standards, telling us to be "perfect, as your heavenly Father is perfect," saying, be loving to all, even your enemies, make peace with all. Yet, Jesus also acknowledges sin, saying if someone sins deliberately and cruelly, harming those God loves so much, this is a declaration of war on God himself. But even as Jesus brings out the evil of sin, he tells of his Father's willingness to forgive: "The Son of Man came to seek and to save that which was lost."

Over and over in the gospels we hear Jesus underscore faith, "Your faith has healed you." When the Centurion asks him to heal his servant, saying he knows all he has to do is say the word, Jesus' response is remarkable: "Truly I tell you, in no one in Israel have I found such faith." He cures the woman with the hemorrhage, saying "Your faith has made you well," and says the same to the woman from Canaan after he cures her daughter of demons, "Woman, great is your faith." He teaches that even small faith, the size of a mustard seed, can move mountains.

So many times Jesus speaks of faith, and what does he mean by this? What kind of faith did those people have that moved Jesus so deeply? It was faith *in him*. These were people who somehow trusted that what Jesus was doing was the same as if God in heaven were doing it. All Jesus said or did was the working out of everything he had learned from the Father in heaven. There he was, a living messenger from heaven, and some people—even outsiders—believed him. When he got affirmation like this, he could continue with joy and hope in his mission—that he had come to present his Father to the world so that people could know God as he really is. "I and the Father are one," he proclaims, giving an astounding new definition of faith—know me and be like me and you, too, will be one with us. Be like *him*? That would mean to be loving, forgiving, peaceful, not steeped in anger or revenge, generous, never hypocritical, accepting of all—even strangers and those who are different from yourself—thankful for food, flowers, birds, water, concerned enough for others in need to share your wealth with them, and then—to humbly gather in fellowship to proclaim this message.

Jesus redefined faith, but he left us no set formulas, knowing all individuals would have to discover for themselves how to bring this faith to the world they would be born into. Faith, for Jesus, meant that we were being set free so we could get to know who we are and who we should be. He knew that this meant all who internalized this faith would be trail blazers in their own lifetimes, always on the move to understand and explore how they were to live out this faith in their times, in the midst of history ever in the making.

Back in 1966, in the era of Vatican II, I had the good fortune to attend a conference on Contemporary Theology at Loyola College in Montreal, Canada. The "faculty" that week was a trio of really distinguished academics, Father Hans Kung, and Protestant theologians Martin Marty and Harvey Cox. All three, in their own way, pointed out that Christianity had taken a dramatic step forward in identifying itself with humanity, no longer relying on the fear of hell or the hope of heaven.

"The Spirit is asking today, what does it mean to be a man in this earthly sphere, and theology is advancing in the direction of helping the Church serve the world," said Father Kung. "The 'aggiornamento' Christian accepts this commitment of loving the world—which means to be servant, not exploiter—in freedom and sacrifice, paralleling the earliest Christians who were God's avant garde in the commitment of contradicting the times and recklessly loving one another—to the death."

Then Father Kung emphasized that "The function of the Church is the calling of the world to faith—with faith defined as making *a radical decision for God in confrontation with our neighbor.* This is way beyond the notion of individual salvation."

I believed then and still do that this definition of faith precisely summarizes how Jesus wanted us to carry on his life, always reading the signs of the times, becoming involved, or at least concerned over, the crucial areas of need in our span of years. In my lifetime I have met and worked with so many people who lived their faith with their sleeves pulled up, believing:

—the time had come to say "enough" to the abuse of people based on the color of their skin; no Christian could sit back and do nothing while interracial justice was blocked by long-standing prejudice; we marched with Jesus for civil rights for all, and the work goes on;

—the time had come to take poverty out of the shadows and hear all the cries for the alleviation of suffering, from starvation and homelessness to loneliness, and the work goes on;

—the time had come to plead for peace in a world which now could see the end of civilization from the horrendous weapons we've developed, and the work goes on;

—the time had come for the religions of the world to come together, seeking an understanding of their differences so that serious crises would not develop over dogmatic differences, and the work goes on. . . .

Hans Kung did something for me that week, nearly forty years ago, that falls into the definition of what it is that a teacher does. He opened my mind to consider new possibilities about old teachings, one of them "revelation." Up to that point I had followed the teaching presented to us that all revelation has been completed and ended with the death of the last apostle, John. To me, it had always seemed inadequate to expect that we could find all the answers needed for new ethical problems brought on by new centuries, technological societies, and melting-pot cultures in the stated teachings of the church.

For example, did our theology cover the meaning of a "just war" in a nuclear age, the justification of using a machine to prolong physical life, the right of poor nations to share the bounty of rich nations, the meaning of equal opportunity, a guaranteed annual income, and proper use of leisure, and issues like sexual relationships in overpopulated countries and the priesthood for women?

Father Kung made the point that "new interpretations" are inevitable. "The whole event of salvation began with Jesus Christ. . . . We are to continually translate the original message to present needs and use all the events in between to help. . . . We cannot stop thinking because something is defined. Re-interpretation has to go on."

He explained this was not implying that anything new was being added to the original message. It was more that the original message was still being discovered. He likened this to walking into a dark room and turning on a lamp. The area around the lamp would be disclosed to you and you could believe that you now had seen everything in that room. But suppose another light went on, disclosing yet some other furnishings in that room. Your knowledge and vision would then be greatly broadened because now you had more information about that room.

Father Kung proposed that the "room"—the original message—no doubt held much more than we yet realized and that only as many more "lights" are turned on with the passage and progress of centuries will we discover ever more of the mysteries and truth of the message. His careful distinction between revelation and interpretation made much sense to me, particularly his restatement that "Revelation is the action of God on mankind. Therefore, revelation is not 'closed.' This is not to say there is new revelation, but rather new interpretations because of new demands of the original message."

I think this falls into a commentary made by Jesus in his day that he would have us remember. It was when the Pharisees and Sadducees demanded a sign from heaven to test his truthfulness. He told them, I would guess perhaps cynically, "You know how to interpret the appearance of the sky, but you cannot interpret the signs of the times." The fact that Jesus used that specific expression means it relates to faith, putting an importance on our need to be aware of "the signs of the times." Everything relating to God—who is one with us—is current and needs our attention. That's faith—and Jesus told us so.

He never promised, though, that believing in all he said and did was going to put us on the easy path in life. I can relate more stories than I'd like to acknowledge about how good people, who embrace the faith of Jesus, suffer blows, from minor to earth-shaking. I remember once when a friend stopped by my house, just to have me wipe her tears. Helen's husband was the head grounds keeper for a community college, until a pole fell, struck his head, fracturing his skull, and landed on his neck, cracking a vertebra. That same week her son lost his job, and then she began having severe abdominal pain and had to spend a week in the hospital for testing to try to find the cause. "Why did all this happen to me?" she asked, crying.

I had already learned that when people are hurting badly, they really don't want answers; they simply need to be hugged. It's the human connection they're really asking for. So I didn't answer, only tried to comfort her. But that evening I happened to pick up a book I had just purchased, called *A Retreat For Lay People*, written by Msgr. Ronald Knox. In one chapter he dealt with this condition of life—where you get up in the morning and first your shoe string breaks, then you trip and wrench your back on the way to the bathroom, your coffee spills, burning your hands and ruining your clothes, etc., etc. Then he comments on these moments in life by asking, "Well, why shouldn't they happen to us?"

I think he may have been trying to point out that something wacky has settled into our approach to life. We *expect* that only good things should happen to us. We feel entitled to have a smooth ride on this earth, and when we hit roadblocks and blowouts, we are almost astonished. Msgr. Knox speculates that's naivete. Cars will break down; storms will damage houses; jobs will be lost; people will be out to steal from you; bad things will happen, along with the good. So to ask, "Why is this happening?" becomes the wrong question, the priest-author points out. The right questions would be, "Why shouldn't I expect that a number of bad or annoying things will happen to me many times over in life?" Given the reality of living, the path is going to be rough, and we should spend our efforts not in fretting, but in moving on.

I thought that was good stuff when I read it in my much younger days. I felt a good Christian didn't dally with self-pity, but went moving on. And I still do. But when I started to meet people with indescribable tragedy, and came to know that degree of pain myself, I didn't expect answers; there weren't any. I needed compassion. I reread the gospels and was struck by the recurring stories of how Jesus cured the hurting. He put his hands on them, he cried, he lifted them up, even, in the case of a child and a friend, from the dead. Jesus was showing us how his Father suffers with us, and also the true healing that can come if we only trust in him.

Some people in their lifetimes have incredible sufferings that bring them to this trust, like the French poet Jacques Riviere. He knew human desperation when he was a prisoner for four years during World War I, but from his great suffering, he found himself "truly thrown to God." He believed God had visited him in prison and learned that God would always be revealed "in his grace. Grace, like water flowing under the ground for a long time, suddenly bursts the surface here and there, runs over, covers everything." Yet later, Riviere also knew that he would be "swallowed up again in the life where a thousand human traces confuse God's footsteps within him." He knew he would not always soar with those wonderful moments "when God . . . instead of inviting us, he calls us. He occupies us." And so he wrote a note and underscored the role of the will in faith, reminiscent of the plea, "I believe, Lord, help my unbelief."

Only a poet can see images like "thrown to God," and "He occupies us" in describing personal faith. Fidelity won out in Jacques Riviere, for his life affirmed that "God's footsteps are not effaced on our inner roads; we cover them with dust or mud, but they are not wiped out." Still, for so many, when life becomes confusing, and racked with troubles and losses, unfairness, and loss, it takes an act of will to hold on to faith.

We may wish that Jesus said a bit more about why his Father set up the world the way he did, why there is so much disruption, evil, and tragedy, along with goodness. But he didn't, and that's the way it is. I asked my son Peter once, when I was praying, why there has to be so much pain in this world. I clearly heard him respond, with no inflection or explanation, "There's pain in God." This brought back what Meister Eckhart said, "How ever great one's suffering is . . . God suffers from it first." Then, more to the point, Peter added, "There's love in God." That brought me right back to the Jesus, with the cross in his heart, who beckoned to me so

I would follow him in a lifelong exploration to understand his definition of faith while I was plagued with mystery.

This was never a journey to be taken alone. Jesus made it so very clear that God's love is expressed in how we share that love with each other. I heard a talk once by an Orthodox theologian who used the story of the miracle of the loaves and fishes to describe the mystery, the power, and the potential for mutual nourishing when believers come together as a community. He said when people gather for the common cause of faith, they become a community in which grace multiplies. By coming together *they become a sum greater than its parts.* Like the bread and fishes, the nourishment is continuous and complete, with leftovers.

"God can show himself as He really is only to real men. And that means not simply to men who are individually good, but to men who are united together in a body, loving one another, helping one another, showing Him to one another," C. S. Lewis wrote. "For that is what God meant humanity to be like; like players in one band, or organs in one body. Consequently, the one really adequate instrument for learning about God is the whole Christian community, waiting for Him *together.* Christian brotherhood is, so to speak, the technical equipment for this science—the laboratory outfit."

Jesus wanted all people from his day and forever to live by the faith he redefined. His own words testify to that:

Everyone who hears these words of mine and does them will be like a wise man who built his house upon the rock; and the rain fell, and the floods came, and the winds blew and beat upon that house, but it did not fall, because it had been founded on the rock. And everyone who hears these words of mine and does not do them will be like a foolish man who built his house upon the sand; and the rain fell, and the floods came, and the winds blew and beat against that house, and it fell; and great was the fall of it.

Conclusion

*My sisters, doesn't it seem to you
that God wants to make use of you?*

—St. Vincent de Paul

(to the Daughters of Charity)

Never can I forget a spring day in 1960 when my then husband decided to teach me a lesson. He had studied to be a Jesuit priest, and had come away with some rather strange ideas about how he could force people to be holy, according to his definition of holiness. I was to be in for a surprise that day, and quite a bit of sadness.

I had been busy with the nonstop tasks I had to accomplish every day to keep my children, then ranging in age from two to ten, well fed, well clothed, and well occupied, and our house clean. Since I could never keep track of where their father was, I didn't know he had gone into the attic. As for why? He had apparently decided to confiscate all my belongings from my youthful days that I had stored there. These were an assortment of belongings I had kept after my marriage, and I regarded them as precious to no one else but me.

There was my wedding gown, which I had made myself, and saved so that one day maybe a daughter would wear it for her own wedding. Most precious, was the large box of letters my Uncle Augie had written to me during World War II, when he served four years in the Coast Guard. We had had a very special relationship since I was a child, and do, to this day, where, thank God, he is now, as he says, "Ninety-three and counting." His letters to me, so detailed, were actually literature, and I had planned one day to put these together as a cherished book. I also had a large amount of firsthand material on World War II, newspapers with the huge black headlines telling of major events, magazine articles, posters, fliers, and other souvenirs. I saved these thinking that one day I might have children who would appreciate these "historical," firsthand records of that war.

Among my belongings were copies of the first of my published writings when I was a teenager, most of them in newspapers, including *The Evangelist*, the diocesan paper that back then carried a page in each issue about Catholic school news. I also had saved some crocheted doilies that I had made when I was ten, some embroidered handkerchiefs, some books I considered precious, bought in a used book store with hard earned money. I even had a little box with a lock of my hair, given to me by my mother who had cut my curls when I was four, and then saved one to keep for me. I wanted that curl to give to whichever daughter would believe it was really my hair, since it was golden, more blonde than the brown-haired mother they knew!

Well, that day, my one time husband confiscated all my belongings from my youth and burned them. He did this to make sure I learned that I was never supposed to care about "material things," some version of "holiness" he had apparently latched on to that applied to others, not himself. I was quite devastated about losing the items I considered precious, particularly my Uncle Augie's letters and my golden curl, but I wasn't going to let the anger get to me, which I have long admitted is some kind of a joke, considering that a half a lifetime later, I'm still talking about it!

What I do remember, though, is running up to the bedroom. I had a few moments of panic, worrying that he might have also removed my picture of Jesus that I had always had on the wall by my side of the bed. If that was gone, I knew I could not take this "lesson" lightly. I was overjoyed when I saw it was still there. Apparently, he had forgotten, or simply overlooked, that I had something from my past on the wall in the bedroom.

Perhaps the reason I've never forgotten that day and those losses is precisely because I didn't lose what was most valuable and important to me. I felt this was another affirmation that Jesus was never going to let me forget that he was permanently there for me, as his beckoning proved. I never stopped searching, with prayer and study, to understand what it meant to take his hand, and Jesus helped me learn a better lesson that day than not being "attached to material things."

It began with a question—could I recognize him in all the people who disturb us, who are cruel and certainly unlovable? Like it or not we rub shoulders and bounce head-on with others all day long, many of whom disturb our inner peace. I had to learn that Jesus wanted me to know that we are not at all like him if we build walls around us to protect ourselves from the unlovables. If we resist these difficult ones with anger, the world can become an insane place. If we respond with love, then order can return and our lives, and the world, can make sense again, with conflict over and peace restored. Jesus said "See me" in all the people we would avoid, ignore, condemn, throw aside, hate—

precisely so that we could see clearly that we must love them, too, or peace is never possible in our lives or in the world.

This was the code I would have to choose to live by if I held on to Jesus' hand. It was another affirmation, as I have continually learned over the years, that in spite of my oftentimes weakness and failures, my life would be shaped by Jesus.

Sometimes I would feel I had been given some special instructions, like when I read about the life of St. Vincent de Paul, a saint who is credited with no miracles, who never claimed to see a heavenly vision, but who spent his life responding to the real and multiple needs of the poor and the suffering. He had helped some good women found a religious order, rightfully called the Daughters of Charity, and, in a sentence to them, explained what heavenly beckoning is all about: "Doesn't it seem to you that God wants to make use of you?"

Actually, yes. I believe God wanted to make use of me when he chose me to bring new life into his world, blessed with a condition called motherhood. I discovered that to have been called upon to share in this creative service—that stems from and is linked to heaven itself—is a grace that defies description. If I could love my babies so much, I could really understand the love God has for his children.

I had gotten a clue about mother's love when I was very young, from my grandmother, who had eight children. She lived a hundred miles away from us but we often visited her. One morning when I was at her house, I saw her pouring corn flakes for my then twenty-seven-year-old Uncle Joe. That struck me as strange, because I was only seven, and I poured my own corn flakes. I asked her if she did that because she loved Uncle Joe more than her other seven children.

She shook her head, held up her hand, with her fingers spread, and asked me, in her broken English, "Which finger, if you cut it off, does not hurt?"

I got the point. I was a bit older, of course, before I got the message—that your children always remain part of you, like the fingers of your hand. My grandmother didn't know I'd never forget what she told me that day, but something about that image stayed permanently with me. It was when I had my own children and understood love in a completely new way, from how my breath and my heartbeats were no longer independent, and how these young ones were as much a part of me as the fingers on my hand, that I really understood what my grandmother was telling me that long ago day. I would wonder sometimes, knowing how much I loved my children, if God could possibly love any of us more. And then I would think, "yes, of course," for God is our parent, needing us to do God's work on earth. Truly, we are his fingers, and I could understand how much it would hurt God if even one of us were cut off from him.

Having children put me in intimate touch with Jesus, who radiated joy when he was around the little ones. You can't help smiling when you see the charm and energy of children, and I have so many memories, like still seeing flashbacks of my daughter Margee as a tot, always laughing and so bubbly that I used to call her my human pogo stick. I could tell so many stories about my children when they were youngsters that make me marvel at the wisdom of children. One very special one was a conversation I had with my son Francis Xavier, when he was all of five years old. He was playing with a game on the table, and then, out of the blue, looked up and asked me, "Mommy, if I died, would you cry?" I was taken off guard by that, but held my composure, answering, "Of course. Would you cry if I died?" My curly-haired tot thought a minute and then said, "I won't cry too hard if you die of old age." I could imagine Jesus smiling broadly at that gem.

When Peter died, I turned to Jesus, sometimes begging, sometimes screaming, needing him to show me the way as I stumbled in new territory, a stranger in a strange land. He never abandoned me, often helping me feel closely in touch with my son, like the early morning of Christmas 1992, our second Christmas without Peter.

It was especially hard to be without Peter that Christmas. I could see him in his red sweats and Santa cap that he always wore on this special day. His presence was so strong that I couldn't stop myself from suddenly sobbing, from the pain of his loss, and the belief that he truly was still here with us.

I soon dried my tears and went into the kitchen to begin some food preparations for the dinner for twelve we would have later. Everyone was still sleeping except for my son-in-law Rick. Because he had gotten up early, he decided to set up the wood in the fireplace in the den for a later fire. The wood I had gotten that year was not well seasoned and it took a lot of coaching to get it started. He had finished and was standing in the doorway between the den and the kitchen, talking to me, as I was busy cutting up vegetables for salad.

We were talking about the O Antiphons and the origins of Christmas and I was saying how glad I am that I have my spiritual anchor, Jesus, whose birthday we were celebrating this day. I told him I had read and investigated a lot of different spiritual practices in the past nearly two years, but all I've learned from this is that I always go back to Jesus. In his words and his life, I find all the beauty and answers that have meaning for me.

At that moment, Rick exclaimed, "Oh, wow! Come here." He pointed to the fireplace. It was a roaring blaze. He said, just as I had given my personal testimony that truth is in Jesus, the fire had spontaneously burst, and he had never put a match to it! It was as if I had received an affirmation from Jesus himself. I never doubted that.

One thing I learned from the difficulties and tragedies of my life was how important it was for me to seek solitude regularly so that I could privately and without distraction bring my confusions to Jesus. Whenever it was possible, I would go to a beach, which I found to be the perfect place for me to do this. When you are in a vast place where earth meets the immensity of water and both meet the endless sky, it has to be as close to paradise as one can get on this earth. For me, this was always a special place to pray.

Once, as I meditating, with the sun caressing me, I became conscious of how sensuous my prayer had become. Sensuous prayer? I had never put those two words together. I was so well taught to be wary of anything that approximated "sensuousness." That word—expressing bodily feeling—was the pathway to soul destruction because it put us on a road going in the opposite direction from Divine things, or so I had been taught long ago.

But on the beach, I could "feel" God. I would reflect on the life and words of his Son Jesus, who could enjoy the sensual feel of oil on his skin—as well as bear the sensual pain of thorns on his head. To follow him meant to relish all good things the Father had given to creation, to seek these out, enjoying the sensuous sight of the lilies and the flying birds of the air. He had a passion for life and this came through strongly in his plea to "be not afraid," and his declaration that he came to set us "free." On the beach, the world seemed to stretch out like a miracle before me and I, relishing the sensual wonder of life, could connect with the powerful lover who had given all this to us.

Sometimes I would confront Jesus on his confusing messages, like "Ask and you shall receive." I could list all the things I had asked for and how I had been ignored. The one thing I became sure of was that I would not receive answers, especially for the tough requests, like "Please, Lord, make my job of living easier." He actually had asked his Father to do the same for him, when, as he knew he was facing torment and death, he cried to his silent Father to please, change the agenda, stop this. I had to reinterpret the "Ask . . . " teaching, once I could accept that rarely do we receive the specific agenda requested. I learned that while we don't "receive" what we specifically ask for, what we do get is tailor-made help from God to get us through whatever it is we're facing. Like it or not, Jesus was living proof that his Father's plan was not to fix things for us but to get us to fix our lives and the world ourselves.

I've been through the hurricanes, the floods, and the volcanoes, and under the sun, the soothing rain, and perfumed breezes. Life always threw its curve balls, some hitting me deeply in the heart. I worked nonstop for my family, my church, my world, and myself. Sometimes the good things in my life would fall under shadows, leaving only a self-pity that would soon disgust me, even as I justified it, whispering that I was only human. But I'm at an age now where I look back at all my difficult life and I say loudly, *no regrets*. I see so clearly that without difficulties in our lives, we can never feel compassion for others. If we don't feel compassion, we have missed the great plea that defined the life of Jesus—that we love one another.

Jesus beckoned, and I took his hand, not knowing at age fifteen, the challenge I accepted when I said yes to his invitation to "Follow me." He was a radical, presenting a message like nothing ever heard before, teaching that God and humans are connected in an intimate way. He altered all the accepted "eye for an eye" kind of teachings people had long accepted to show everyone, then and now, that they were supposed to think and act in a radically different way—in truth,

God's way. He respected women, and bypassing male attitudes of the day, regarded them as intelligent people who were as privy to his teachings as were men. Jesus came to "show us how to make the world right" and didn't plan to preach and move on. He came to stay forever. He beckons to us with a hard offer. You follow me and I'll give you a heart transplant so you can be me.

That's the Jesus who shaped my life, and I'm not alone. I've met so many people who have been Jesus to others, who have carried out his work so strongly that they bring heaven into full view. They have convinced me that until we know Jesus, we have little chance of understanding the grandeur of which we are capable— and our true destiny, so well expressed by C. S. Lewis:

> What we have been told is how we can be drawn into Christ—can become part of that wonderful present which the young Prince of the universe wants to offer to his Father—that present which is himself and therefore is us in him. *It is the only thing we were made for.* And there are strange, exciting hints in the Bible that when we are drawn in, a great many things in Nature will begin to come right. The bad dream will be over: it will be morning.

Alleluia and amen!

Resources

Leonardo Boff, *Passion of Christ, Passion of the World*, Orbis, 1987

Dietrich Bonhoeffer, *The Martyred Christian* (Selected by Joan W. Brown), Macmillan Publishing Co., 1983

Marcus J. Borg, *Meeting Jesus Again for the First Time*, HarperSanFrancisco, 1994

Carlo Carretto, *In Search of the Beyond*, Orbis, 1976

G.K. Chesterton, *Orthodoxy*, Ignatius Press, 1995 (John Lane Co., 1905)

Thomas C. Clark and Hazel D. Clark, Editors, *Christ in Poetry*, Association Press, 1952

Henri Daniel-Rops, *Jesus and His Times*, E.P. Dutton & Co., 1954

Jacques Delarue, *The Holiness of Vincent de Paul*, P.J. Kennedy & Sons, 1960

M. Fielder and L. Rabben, Editors, *Rome Has Spoken*, Crossroad Publishing, 1998

Jim Forest, *Mother Maria Skobtsova*, Orbis, 2003

Victor Gollancz, *Man and God*, Houghton Mifflin Co., 1951

T.R. Glover, *The Jesus of History*, Grosset & Dunlap, 1917

Alban Goodier, *The Public Life of Our Lord Jesus Christ*, P.J. Kennedy & Sons, 1944

Andrew Greeley, *The Jesus Myth*, Doubleday & Co., 1971

William Hamilton, *A Quest for the Post-Historical Jesus*, Continuum, 1994

Alden Hatch, *A Man Named John*, Hawthorn Books, 1963

C. S. Lewis, *Mere Christianity*, Macmillan Publishing Co., 1943

C. S. Lewis, *Miracles*, Macmillan Publishing Co., 1947

C. S. Lewis, *Surprised by Joy*, Harcourt Brace Jovanovich, 1956

Robert Llewelyn, Editor, *Julian, Woman of Our Day*, Twenty-Third Publications, 1987

Francois Mauriac, *Proust's Way*, Philosophical Library, 1950

Fulton Oursler, *The Greatest Story Ever Told*, Doubleday, 1949

Giovanni Papini, *The Life of Christ*, Harcourt Brace & Co., 1923

D. Philips, E. Howes, L. Nixon, *The Choice Is Always Ours*, Harper & Row San Francisco, 1989

John F. Pollard, *The Unknown Pope, Benedict XV and the Pursuit of Peace*, Geoffrey Chapman Publishers, 1999

Adelaide A. Procter, *Poetical Works*, A. L. Burt Publisher, 1865

Claudio Rendina, *The Popes, Histories and Secrets*, Seven Locks Press, 2002

John Shea, *The Challenge of Jesus*, The Thomas More Press, 1984

Chad Walsh, *Behold the Glory*, Harper & Brothers,1955

N. T. Wright, *Jesus and the Victory of God*, Fortress Press, 1996

N. T. Wright, *The New Testament and the People of God*, Fortress Press, 1992

ANTOINETTE BOSCO has written "The Bottom Line" for the Catholic News Service since 1974. She was formerly the executive editor of *The Litchfield County Times* and wrote for *The Long Island Catholic* for eleven years. She served on the Suffolk County, Long Island Human Rights Commission and was a faculty and staff member at State University of New York at Stony Brook. She's written more than 250 magazine articles and was honored in 2002 with a Christopher Award and a Pax Christi award for *Choosing Mercy, A Mother of Murder Victims Pleads to End the Death Penalty,* which also received wide critical acclaim. *One Day He Beckoned* is her eleventh book. She lives in Brookfield, Connecticut.